Giving Up God

"In *Giving Up God*, Sarah Henn Hayward moves from a binary world with rigid boundaries to a place much messier and muddier—sometimes literally—with room for big questions with no pre-packaged answers. Her ever-broadening worldview echoes Mark Twain's observation that 'travel is fatal to prejudice, bigotry, and narrow-mindedness.' Hayward's writing is compassionate, kind, and generous, and her work left this progressive Christian filled with wonder, embracing mystery, and grateful for the opportunity to explore the terrain through which she gently guides us."

—Cynthia Vacca Davis, author of *Intersexion*

"Sarah Hayward's debut gives us a tender yet provocative deconversion testimony. With great compassion and kindness for everyone still embracing faith, she yet raises all her questions and, yes, bold complaints without flinching: Where is God in moments of gross injustice? How could a universe-creator who is both all-powerful and all-good come up with the terribly flawed reality we all know? We all have different answers—or maybe none at all—for questions like these, but Sarah gives us the intimate opportunity to see and understand exactly how she came to her own conclusions—conclusions which, if the popular Christian deconstruction movement is any indication, are likely held in similar fashion by many in our midst. Insight into these stories is a gift, one that Sarah offers with genuine sincerity and care for all invested in the conversation."

—Stephanie Eagleson, writer of "Autopsy of Abuse"

"It wasn't very far into Sarah's book when I realized I was reading my own story. Even though everyone's path is uniquely theirs, there are similarities common among all deconstruction journeys, and Sarah describes these in a beautiful way. What stands out the most, though, is her courage to put everything at risk and ask the hard questions. The result is she discovers herself and who she may be in the world, as well as a deeper connection to the ones she loves and the universe. If you are deconstructing, questioning your beliefs, and your relationship to religion and the church, read this book for encouragement and validation. But also read it to find a new companion on your spiritual pilgrimage."

—David Hayward, NakedPastor,
author of *Flip It Like This!*

Giving Up God

Resurrecting a Spirituality of Love and Wonder

Sarah Henn Hayward

LAKE DRIVE
lakedrivebooks.com

Lake Drive Books
6757 Cascade Road SE, 162
Grand Rapids, MI 49546

info@lakedrivebooks.com
lakedrivebooks.com
@lakedrivebooks

Publishing books that help you heal, grow, and discover.

Paperback ISBN: 978-1-957687-30-8
eBook ISBN: 978-1-957687-32-2

Library of Congress Control Number: 2023943703

This book is a memoir. It reflects the author's present recollections and information gathering of experiences over time. Some of the names of individuals or institutions and their characteristics have been changed, some events have been compressed, and some dialogue has been recreated.

All Scripture quotations, unless otherwise indicated, are taken from the ESV® Bible (The Holy Bible, English Standard Version®), copyright © 2001 by Crossway, a publishing ministry of Good News Publishers. Used by permission. All rights reserved. The ESV text may not be quoted in any publication made available to the public by a Creative Commons license. The ESV may not be translated in whole or in part into any other language.

Sherrie Lovler and Anthony Lawlor. "The Long Road Here." In *Two as One: Poems from a New Love*. Santa Rosa: Ink Monkey Press, 2007. Reprinted with Permission.

Cover design by Mietta Yans
Photo by Laura Vinck, Unsplash

This book is dedicated to all the seekers, the curious, the believers and the doubters, the embracers of the mysterious, the bold and brave who aren't afraid to question the status quo, who aren't afraid to question everything. This is for the wonderers, the wanderers, the wild and authentic humans brave enough to live into their own truth.

Contents

Introduction

WELCOME, READER. I'M SO HONORED that you are here. Before diving in, I want to be clear about the message of this book and my intentions. This book is the story of my faith journey in reverse, beginning as an earnest, devout, born-again Christian and evolving into an atheistic poetic naturalist, or maybe a Christian atheist, or simply an agnostic. I am certainly no longer a Christian in the classic sense of the word.

My journey was lonely, so I wrote the book I wish I'd had to help me walk through it all. As you will discover, I am a massive bibliophile and look to books not only for entertainment, but also for knowledge, growth, and assurance that I am not alone in my views. I know atheists I could turn to for guidance, but they don't come from such a strong faith background and can't relate to the grief I am experiencing. I know plenty of progressive, forward-thinking Christians, but they can't relate to completely walking away from any concept of a Higher Being. This book is niche to that specific formerly-faithful, now seriously-questioning person who isn't quite sure where to go or what to think. My goal is to be a source of comfort and camaraderie for anyone who had a deep faith and has left it behind.

This book is *not* trying to convince anyone to join me. That has been one of the gifts of leaving my faith. I no longer have a constant, underlying compulsion to change everyone's mind and behavior to match my own. Being an evangelical, Protestant Christian meant I always had converting others on my mind, even as I became more progressive. In my earlier Christian days I tried to steer conversations with unsuspecting neighbors and nonreligious friends toward Jesus whenever possible. My neighbor Matt was over one day when we were nine years old, and as we were heading outside to play, I trapped him in the mudroom with a passionate explanation of the love of God. Leaning up against the washing machine, I teared up as I sold my story while he looked on like a deer in the headlights.

As my faith grew and changed, I stopped believing in the effectiveness of hostage witnessing or knocking on strangers' doors to talk about God (as I was forced to do while in Campus Crusade during college). I gravitated toward St. Francis of Assisi's philosophy to "preach the gospel at all times and if necessary, use words." I stopped trying to convert people to Christianity at any and every opportunity, but I still wanted to impact folks' spiritual lives and inspire them to change.

I thought my worldview was right and that of others was wrong and needed to change. I felt responsible for bringing about that change. It was exhausting and a little scary. I constantly worried that I wasn't doing enough.

Not only was I afraid of allowing my loved ones to end up in hell, but I was constantly worried that I wasn't living my life in a way that would truly please God. Jesus had harsh words when people asked how to follow him: sell all your possessions, leave your family behind. I had a closet full of clothes and a (small) bank account balance. I wasn't dedicating every minute of every day to the service of my Lord. Was I a disappointment to God? In the Bible, Jesus told a terrifying parable involving sheep and goats. Both groups were caught off guard when Jesus praised the sheep for feeding the hungry, clothing the naked, and visiting the prisoner while he banished the goats to eternal fire for neglecting to do those things. Jesus said serving "the least of these" people is in fact serving God directly, and neglecting to do so would result in separation from God.[1] Was I doing enough to avoid being a goat?

Then, in 2005, I received an email from my college pastor that I held onto for years. I had written to ask him to spell it out for me specifically: how should *I* follow God in my daily interactions? I fretted that my life felt too normal; I was just going to church, going to class, reading my Bible, and hanging out with my friends. Didn't I need some sort of ceremony, some way to obviously dedicate each day to God?

My pastor's response basically told me to relax, that God would put people and opportunities in my path as he* saw fit, and that I could simply go about living my life. That response was my hall pass. I kept it for years, craving permission to live my life as it happened without the threat of God leering over my shoulder and judging. I didn't entirely

---

* A side note on pronouns: I will be using different pronouns for God throughout the book to coincide with my changing views. The God of my childhood and early adult years was very much male, so I'm using he/him/his when telling a story from that time. Since my idea of God expanded and I realized that the God of the Bible professed to contain both the male and female image and even used female analogies to describe themselves, I avoid pronouns or use they/them for God.

trust my pastor's advice, not yet. I kept worrying that I wasn't living a radical enough life for God. I didn't feel comfortable taking each day as it came until I stopped believing in religion altogether.

It has been a massive relief to feel that evangelical pressure slide off my back. Without the threat of eternal damnation for unbelieving loved ones hanging over me anymore, I'm allowed to let others live their lives however they choose without it affecting me. Without God constantly watching from the eaves, I can stop agonizing over how to win God's favor each day.

I do not begrudge anyone their faith. Whatever motivates anyone to live a healthy, fulfilling life sounds great to me! My aim here is not to get Christians or any other people of faith to renounce their beliefs and agree that I am right. I *am* a firstborn child with a thriving ego, so I do love being right, but I am honestly not concerned with that anymore as far as spirituality or religious beliefs (or the lack thereof) go. I am still open to changing my mind. I have not landed in an immutable new philosophy or theology, nor would I want to force my current worldview upon anyone else.

If anything I say here makes you question your reality and think new thoughts, I truly hope that your faith is strong enough to handle it. If you are already questioning every last thing down to the nature of the universe, then you might find some relief hearing my story and knowing that you aren't alone. Regardless of what you think comes next, most of us agree that we only get one life to live on this planet. Let's make the most of every moment.

My Testimony

A PERSON'S TESTIMONY IS THE story of how they came to be a Christian. The best testimonies were artfully delivered, sharing their story in the most dramatic way possible. I—a pious goody-two-shoes for the first seventeen years of my life—was always jealous of the bad boys who hit rock bottom before God saved them. They got to have fun before dramatically walking away from all that to become good. Lucky! I was born bowing my head in prayer and holding a devotional. My fun times came later as gradually, over the last twenty years, I began to challenge my rigid views. I tiptoed further and further away from the land of my beliefs to eventually arrive in an entirely new territory outside of religion altogether.

I was raised in the evangelical church by Christian parents. They both came from religious families, but neither one took it too seriously in their youth or felt that they had a personal relationship with Christ (the backbone of the evangelical experience). My mom had her born-again conversion moment while attending Central Michigan University through a friend who was involved in Campus Crusade for Christ. Engaged to my dad at the time, and with the fervor of a fresh convert, my mother tried to get him to "pray the prayer" as well. He was not thrilled but agreed that they could pick out a church together for the sake of unity in their marriage. Sometime later, a powerful altar call experience at church compelled him to go all-in for Christ. He became the parent who woke us all up by obnoxiously belting out "How Great Thou Art" in the morning. My parents are genuinely grateful for their faith—it gives their lives purpose and value. That's the faith they passed along to me.

The concept of original sin—that everyone is born wretched and sinful and is worthless on their own outside of Christ—was not a driving factor in my brand of Christianity. I always held onto the fact that God first created humans and said "it was very good."[2] Believing that the Creator of the universe knew and loved me personally gave me a strong sense of worth, a high regard for my value in the world, and a deep knowledge that I am lovable and loved. I believed that God—who made everything and knew everyone—cared about my life specifically and loved me for being me, despite my flaws. I believed it when I was told that Jesus sacrificed his life for me and erased my sin. Not that I couldn't commit new sins—because, of course, "none is righteous, no, not one"[3]—but that Jesus's sacrifice made it possible for God to forgive me for whacking my brother and gossiping with friends from school and love me anyway.

My life was drastically impacted, spiritually and physically, when I was nine years old. I underwent a routine physical before attending summer camp, and the doctor discovered a hump on my back, diagnosing me with scoliosis. X-rays revealed advanced curvatures that made an "S" shape in my spine. "S for Sarah!" I used to proclaim. Not only did I have scoliosis, but I had an additional and unrelated spinal problem called spondylolisthesis (try saying that at nine years old!), which was even *more* severe. A section of my spine was slipping forward off the column of vertebrae, threatening to crush the vertebra below and potentially sever the spinal nerves at that level. I was young enough to assume what was happening to me was a somewhat normal occurrence, and I didn't get too worried. I did get upset when my ballet and gymnastics careers came to a screeching halt and when I was put in a back brace for twenty-three hours a day, seven days a week. My torso was wrapped in rigid plastic and metal to attempt to stop the curves from getting worse.

I *hated* the brace. The stiff plastic didn't breathe, making me constantly sweaty, and it was bulky under my clothes. Most of my shirts ended up with little holes where the screws from the brace wore them out. I tried to make the most of it and would taunt boys at school into punching my belly, claiming I did one thousand sit-ups a day and had abs of steel. They only fell for that trick once.

Entering junior high school, when everyone is desperately trying to fit in, and comparing my bulky torso to the other girls' lithe bodies was painful. I stared at their backs in class and daydreamed about what it would feel like if my back were so straight and smooth. I certainly had my pity parties, lamenting the discomfort of how I both looked and felt. My parents were as supportive as possible. Whenever I'd cry about my circumstances, my mom would look so pained and express her wish to trade places with me. But I was learning to deal with the fact that life isn't always easy, a useful lesson that would come in handy again.

My parents kept signing me up for as many normal activities and sports as I wanted. Anything involving too much bending and flexibility was out, but I played tennis and softball and was even on my school's cheerleading squad, wearing my brace under all my uniforms. My doctor did not love this fact. He listened skeptically as I begged to do all the activities I wanted to do and my mom fought hard to keep my childhood as "normal" as possible. He took some real convincing to approve of the cheerleading squad. We reassured him that this was not the athletic stunts-and-tosses version of cheerleading but in reality more of a glorified clapping section for the school basketball team. He granted his begrudging support.

One summer my family vacationed at a fancy KOA campground in the Appalachian Mountains that had a pool. I had to put my back brace on over my bathing suit—twenty-three hours a day, remember!—and was quite embarrassed about it. As I was swimming and sensing people staring at me, another little girl entered the pool with the help of her mother. Looking back, I can see that she likely had cerebral palsy; her limbs were awkwardly contorted. She wasn't verbal, but she was clearly having a fantastic time in the water, happily grunting and smiling with her whole face.

Watching everyone's eyes swivel over to her and stop staring at me made an impression. I felt humbled, realizing that while I did look different, my brace was normally able to stay hidden and didn't interfere with every aspect of my life. The experience gave me a healthy dose of perspective and taught me to stay positive and make the most of my situation, handling life as it came.

Dealing with scoliosis never caused me to question God. Being so young, I wasn't asking any hard questions of God yet. I kept praying that I would be cured, not thinking much of it when my curvatures continued to advance. There's a verse Christians like to quote when life is hard: "God is faithful, and he will not let you be tempted beyond your ability."[4] I trusted that God would either fix me or make me strong enough to handle my struggles.

Though I wore the brace for three years, twenty-three hours a day (basically only taking it off to shower), my curvatures continued advancing and became frighteningly severe. The slipping spondylolisthesis kept advancing as well. My doctor determined that I needed surgery as soon as I hit puberty and had completed my major growth spurts. Imagine the excitement of waiting for your first period with the added awareness of highly invasive, risky spinal surgeries right around the corner! Weeks after I turned twelve years old, two major surgeries were scheduled.

At the time, I attended a small, Christian private school, and the school ran a 24-hour prayer vigil for me during the operations. I was under the knife for over ten hours while the surgeon—after being harassed by my mom into doing both surgeries at once—fixed each of my issues in one sitting. Afterward, I recovered in the hospital for over a week, quickly learning to walk and use the stairs again with the help of physical therapists. My room was flooded with cards, balloons, bouquets of flowers, and visitors from school and church. I received so many get-well cards that my dad hung strips of double-sided tape from the ceiling with cards stuck along them. Columns of well-wishes from ceiling to floor.

I was thrilled to have the surgery because it meant I was finally out of the brace. The brace was Enemy Number One. I was nervous the night before surgery—I recall running up and down the hallways of the hotel near the hospital with jittery energy—but I was completely on board for this permanent solution. With the added bonus of missing school and all the presents I received, surgery felt like a party after suffering from the brace for so long.

My recovery was smooth and swift; I got up to walk within days and moved around well with no major pain or limitations. Visiting my recovery room, my surgeon saw the outpouring of love and prayers from my Christian community. He mused, "There might be something to this prayer stuff. I wonder if God had a hand in your rapid recovery?"

I don't recall feeling a lot of pain (although I did have full access to a morphine drip) and overall, my experience was a pleasant one. Since I had to recover on the spinal floor and not in a pediatric unit, a kind nurse wheeled down a TV/Nintendo cart for my room so I could try out new games and systems that I didn't have at home. I got to miss school. I received presents and positive attention from everyone I knew. One friend's dad even gave me a pair of diamond-studded earrings for handling the whole thing like a champ!

The experience reinforced an internal belief that was developing in me: being a good person, praying, and asking God for what you want worked! I had a serious problem, but it never felt too scary. I successfully responded to surgery, and to this day I haven't suffered from back pain more than any other person. I felt loved and cared for by my community and by God himself. In my bubbled-off little world, God was good, suffering was alleviated if you prayed and asked him for help, and things worked out for the best.

As I advanced through junior high and into high school, I encountered a unique phenomenon that had taken over Christian culture in the early '00s: purity culture. An early clash of ideas between my parents' attitudes versus purity culture showed me there may be other ways of living besides what I was being taught at church. Purity culture was a popular campaign that churches taught to my generation of Christian girls. We were explicitly told that we were responsible for men's actions and that our choices to hug them chest-to-chest, wear revealing clothing, or act even a little flirty would tempt them to lust and commit sin. The concern was not over our safety and welfare, but rather over protecting men and boys from committing a wrongdoing. The church staff routinely talked to the girls in my youth group about our clothing, our actions, the power we held over men, and the responsibility that came with that. We were instructed to only give "side hugs," to never wear spaghetti straps, and to never, *ever* show cleavage, and I internalized that message completely. I was a gatekeeper to stop men from sexual sin.

Being treated like a walking stumbling block made me very nervous about sexual assault. Getting raped was a deep-seated fear of mine. Like many women of my generation, I always looked over my shoulder while walking alone, often holding my keys between my fingers in a fist grip to ward off any potential male attackers. It never even crossed my mind that a man could be or should be held accountable for his own actions regardless of what I was wearing, or saying, or doing with my body.

My parents grew up during the '60s and '70s with relaxed sexual morals and the prolific presence of drugs, and they'd had their fun. As a result, they weren't super uptight or overly controlling in the way that many of my contemporary Christian friends' parents could be. My parents maintained even keels and never got sucked into the unhealthy, shame-driven, manipulative behaviors typically seen in church. Although I was boy-crazy, I did not have any game and did not know how to get a boyfriend. My mom encouraged me to start wearing makeup, and she even tried to get me to loosen up over not ever tempting a guy. She did not observe or understand the pressure I was under during the height of purity culture. Instead, my mom let me know that if I wore a shirt that was the slightest bit sheer and the outline of my bra was a teensy bit visible, that was okay. After all, everyone knew I was wearing a bra anyway, right? But *no*, I thought: a boy could see it and be tempted to want to see more, and I could not be responsible for that!

My dad was a healthy contrast to purity culture as well. He never acted like many of the other dads at our church. He wasn't overly controlling or possessive of me. He didn't jokingly display the shotgun on our mantel when a date came over to pick me up for a school dance—which definitely happened to friends of mine. His unspoken subtext let me know that he trusted me. I never had an official curfew because my parents trusted me to call them if I was going to be home later than expected. They trusted me to use my brain, to be able to read people, and to make my own choices. My dad let me go on dates without needing to interview the guy first.

When I eventually started dating, he never grilled any of my boyfriends, a fact that bothered one guy I dated in college. Nick got to meet my dad when he picked me up to take me back home for a school break and the three of us went out for lunch. My dad is outgoing and gregarious, and he spent the lunch chatting with my boyfriend over sports and tales from his own college days. Nick later told me that he was offended—to him, my dad's failure to rigorously question him meant my dad didn't take our relationship seriously!

Without the rigid behavior code of purity culture being reinforced at home, I started to relax a little and to question the inflexible interpretation of "Christian behavior" I was taught. My parents knew what life was like and what teen-agers were like. They didn't try to stop me from living, and I trusted them and their judgment. I started picking and choosing which church rules to follow. The first rule to break was concerning alcohol.

My closest friends and I decided that we needed to know how we handled alcohol before going away to col-lege, so we concocted a plan. None of us had fake IDs or helpful older siblings, so we gradually pilfered small amounts from my friend's dad's liquor cabinet over a period of weeks so we could practice drinking. We planned a group sleepover at Amy's house as our inaugural drinking party. My first taste of alcohol was a nasty brew of cognac, scotch, and God knows what else, which promptly swirled around my stomach and straight into the toilet. I came home the next morning and told my mom every gruesome detail, including how Amy's mom came to the bathroom to check on me as I was throwing up and I winked at her profusely, letting her know "my medication" (for what?) made me nauseous, nothing more. My mom was grateful that I had spent the night and warned me not to be stupid and drive drunk. No huge overreaction, no punishment. My parents discussed safe drinking habits more around the house, and that was that.

A few months later, I tried marijuana for the first time, intending to spend the night at my friend Amber's house. However, the decision to smoke was a spontaneous one after I had "practiced drinking" with a few beers. The com-bination of beer and pot made my head spin in a way that

I did not enjoy. I slept it off in Amber's room while the party raged on, woke up at 3 a.m., and drove myself home, feeling sober enough. My mom used the opportunity of my being away all night to escape my dad's snoring by sleeping in my bed, so when I crawled in at 3:30, she was there and could smell the stank of pot in my hair. More exasperated for getting woken up than anything else, she admonished me for driving while under the influence and made me promise to be smarter. I realized that it was fun to break some rules but felt convicted to be more careful.

Growing up in an evangelical church during the height of purity culture meant I picked up weird shame complexes about drinking, swearing, and sexuality. After I started drinking those few times my senior year of high school, I guiltily quit on several occasions for prolonged periods. It took me years to get to reach a comfortable, healthy place with drinking. I remained vigilant against swearing. Swearing was a barometer for me, proving if someone was a "real Christian" or not. Real Christians—for the record—didn't swear. I was the most rigid around sexuality, rarely getting into tempting situations and always stopping things before they went too far. I never did more than make out with guys out of a fear of becoming "tainted."

Thankfully, my parents never enforced these messages at home. My mom's secret favorite word was *shit*. My dad was open about his previous drug use. My mom was completely honest about her sexual history prior to my dad. She blew my mind when she said that she didn't feel tainted and used, haunted by past sexual encounters and unable to enjoy intimacy with my father. That is what I was taught to expect at church in too many cheesy examples of flowers with all their petals picked off and "giving away the milk for free." My mom's confession laid some of the first tiny cracks in my rigid understanding of the way things were supposed to be.

My upbringing—which was inherently religious—molded my character in ways I am still proud to own. My parents instilled an ethic in me to be generous and to ask how I can help bear another's burdens. They took my brother and me to soup kitchens on major holidays, supported mission work, and donated to charities in addition to giving to the church. Our family valued a strong work ethic, a humble attitude, a kind heart that stood up for others, and a sense of fun and enjoyment from life.

We took epic vacations across the country in our pop-up camper, turning me into an avid nature lover from a young age. We spent summers exploring the South Carolina coast, the Appalachian Mountains, the Colorado Rockies, and the canyons of Utah and Arizona, and my dad annoyed my brother and me by gushing over the beautiful scenes we would encounter—"You just don't appreciate this the way I do!"

My mom was a constant source of fun and amusement, bending over backward to provide a happy, loving childhood for me and my brother. She chaperoned my seventh grade school trip to Springfield, Illinois, which made a detour to Hannibal, Missouri, to see Mark Twain's boyhood home. We took a steamboat ride on the Mississippi River while there, and my mom startled hilariously at the blast of the steam engine while being filmed for a school project. She promptly won over the hearts of everyone in my class. My mom signed me up for piano lessons and sports teams, carted me around, and made sure I had friends and playdates. She sat through an entire Hanson concert with me and my friend Erika in the late '90s—now that's love! She gave me the massive, priceless gift of a stable, loving childhood.

The faith of my childhood didn't burn me, though I know lots of people whose faith filled them with shame and told them their very bodies were dirty, wrong, and immoral. That wouldn't allow them to enjoy themselves without feeling guilty. That stressed them out to no end with the threat that a fiery eternity must be in their future because the gift of grace was unbelievable. I know that people have suffered immensely under the name of God; have had religious leaders prey upon them, take advantage of them, and abuse them; have been gaslighted and manipulated in horrible, shameful ways. I completely understand why those folks ran far away from Christianity at the first chance they got. Christianity has made lots of enemies. My departure has been more intellectual than personal, as I will share in detail in the pages to come.

I always took my faith seriously. I've read the Bible cover to cover several times over. I maintained a daily journal practice from junior high through college in which I studied the Bible and prayed to God, writing out all my thoughts, feelings, requests, and questions. I've pored over chapters, ruminating on them and analyzing them. I memorized verses and participated in Sunday school, Awana, youth group, and Campus Crusade for Christ. I shared my faith and witnessed to strangers and friends. I've read hundreds of Christian books and Bible studies. I went on a mission trip to Canada the summer before high school. In high school, I preached on stage to my youth group. During college, I led small groups and mentored younger girls through Campus Crusades. I joined a leadership board for the church I attended while in graduate school. I never swore, never kissed a boy until college (wouldn't want to lead them on), and certainly never had sex.

For a long time I followed Christianity while living my life, meeting new people, and enjoying a wide variety of experiences. Over time, however, I began to rub up against uncomfortable inconsistencies. The smooth, unmarred, surface-level faith I had confidently—if naively—skated onto in my youth eventually wore away to reveal bumps and cracks.

It was precisely because I took my faith so seriously and obsessed over it so much that I eventually asked too many questions, ventured way out to where the ice was thin, and fell into the abyss.

Skating Out

When the road
diverged in the wood
and I took the
one less traveled,
Did I know then
of the winding, windy trail,
the mountains to climb,
the crevasses to pass
the alleyways, the demons,
the drifts?

Did I know that the heart aches,
that the path to growth
is not easy,
that the path to joy
can begin by going downhill?

Did I know that the
road is long,
the depths are deep, the
waves are strong,
the mist is mighty?

And if I did,
would I have taken that path?
And if I didn't
would joy have forever
eluded me?

Sherrie Lovler

Exclusion

THE PLANE TOUCHED DOWN ON a hot summer's day—February 14, 2006, Valentine's Day—and I immediately fell in love with Australia. I was fortunate enough to spend a semester abroad during my sophomore year at Marquette University through an exchange program, and I chose Monash University in Melbourne, Australia. I could write a whole book of stories from those five months. Sailing around the Whitsunday Islands, snorkeling the Great Barrier Reef, driving up the Great Ocean Road, traveling over to Fiji for ten glorious days, bushwhacking in the Grampians, and canoeing down the Murray River were just a few of the adventures I experienced.

Raucous times were plentiful on campus. Australians treat drinking like it's the national religion and are always looking to party. Not long after I joined the drinking scene at the end of high school, my Christian guilt became overbearing. I decided to wait until I was of legal age, so during my sophomore year at Marquette, I gave up drinking. However, I was of legal age in Australia, so once I arrived there, I participated without guilt. I became famous for "Sarah Sips"—a way to get around drinking games without becoming completely inebriated. We would often play games in the dorm before heading out for the night, usually involving cards, that required players to take a certain number of drinks after losing their turn. I would have to take up to eight drinks after a bad turn, so I took sips so small that there was barely any liquid in my mouth to swallow.

As much as I let myself off the tight leash and have a little fun, I was still known for being a well-behaved Christian. I immediately sought out the Campus Crusade group at Monash, tried a few churches close to campus, and taped Bible verses on my dorm room wall. At the time I was taken with the story of Hosea, and I copied out several passages from that book for my wall. A friend looking around my room while hanging out noticed the verses. He assumed they were love letters from a boyfriend back home. He was more than a little confused to discover that they were Bible verses.

My dorm hosted a monthly cultural night during which various topics were discussed, often by exchange students. I was asked to lead the informative talk on what Christianity was all about. The evangelical in me was ecstatic. A chance to witness to a captive audience! I tried to play it cool, share the facts, and not get too preachy. I did not tear up this time. Afterward, a few classmates gave me a "good on ya" and a few folks came up to me to say they were surprised to hear all the love talk, expecting more rules and judgment. I explained that there are many varieties of Christians, some more loving than others.

Another week there was a talk from a fellow student about Islam. I attended and was surprised at how similar our messages were. It didn't sound like our beliefs were all that different other than that she referred more to Muhammad than Jesus. Her faith also honored and studied the words of Jesus, the stories of Abraham, and many of the themes I was familiar with from the Bible. She believed in justice for the suffering, care for the poor, and respect for her fellow humans. I learned that *jihad*—often lambasted in the news as a violent terrorist act—is about the struggle against evil and that any good or kind act performed in service of Allah is an act of jihad.

There were many people in my dorm, particularly from Southeast Asia, who practiced Islam. I was floored with the realization that they sounded just like me when discussing their faith. They prayed to God (calling him Allah), studied their scriptures, and tried to live holy lives. If you listened to any of us discuss our faith, it would not be immediately apparent that we followed entirely different religions.

In my ignorance up until that point, I thought that anyone practicing another religion besides Christianity would clearly sound bananas, spouting off obviously false, cult-like ideas. In junior high school I'd read a book called *What's with the Dudes at the Door?* by Kevin Johnson. It taught Christians how to identify all the cultic, false beliefs other religions tried to pass off as true. It was primarily concerned with refuting Mormonism. The message was that evangelical Christianity had figured out the Real Truth and everyone else was wrong. This concept was reinforced at youth group, in church, and in my campus ministry group.

Listening to these pious, deeply faithful Muslim people challenged my views. Not only did they seem to hold many if not all the same values as me, and not only were their lives equally ordered and governed by their faith, but their conviction was as strong as mine.

Could they really be doomed to hell for being on the wrong team?

Did they believe that I was doomed?

LIVING IN THE DORMS WITH both Australians and other exchange students introduced me to friends from cultures and backgrounds entirely new to me. My first weekend in Melbourne, I took the train downtown with four other exchange students: two ladies from Japan and two guys from Malaysia. We went out to eat in Koreatown, and one of the guys ordered food for our whole table. I was the only white person in the entire restaurant, eating new foods and learning to use chopsticks for the first time, getting to know these people who had been raised on the other side of the planet from me. I was overjoyed.

I made friends from countries in Africa, all over Europe, Mexico, Canada, and Southwest Asia. We would stay up late and talk about our different cultural customs—how we celebrated birthdays and big events in our respective communities, what we ate, and what was important. Turns out, most of the rest of the world values soccer much more than Americans. It was so fascinating to hear and so humbling to realize, for the first time really, that there were millions of people around the world living markedly different lives than mine. That my American existence and lifestyle were far from the norm worldwide, not only in terms of religious practices but also in daily existence. I realized that there were many ways to live and behave that were completely normal and acceptable to other groups of people. That sounds obvious, but at the time it was a revelation. It helped me to grow and to realize that the way I lived my life was not the only option available.

One matter that shocked me was the realization that about one third of Australians practice no religion or consider themselves atheists. A professor from my literature class asked the study group one day—in quite a smirking, mocking tone—how many people in the room believed in God. I was one of two people to timidly raise our hands out of the twenty students in the room. Outside of class, my entire friend group on campus wasn't centered around faith as it was back at my home university. There was a Campus Crusade presence that I sought out, but they met during one of my class periods, so I could never attend. I tried a few churches with one of the leaders I met through Cru, but I was honestly more eager to explore the area and have fun adventures as much as possible on the weekends instead of staying in town to go to church.

Spiritually, I was on my own. As I wrestled with my identity in general and my religious identity in particular, finding myself without a strong community of believers to make my views seem standard or "normal," I started asking new questions.

The idea of hell started to rub differently. The Muslim girls I met were soft-spoken, sweet, kind folks who felt like spiritual kindred spirits. How could all these loving, faithful believers—who didn't happen to believe in Jesus as Savior—be banished to suffer for all eternity? Surely there must be another way for a loving God to treat his creation.

To PREPARE FOR MOVING TO Australia, I did what I do best: went to the library and checked out every book, movie, and CD (remember those?) about Australia that I could find. I don't know if my roommate appreciated the didgeridoo music as much as I did. I read the highly entertaining *In a Sunburned Country* by Bill Bryson and was not embarrassed to laugh out loud in public while reading. Books have been a constant presence in my life. According to legend, I started "reading" to my mom at age three because I had memorized my baby board books. Once I started reading in earnest, I never stopped. I read for fun as a child—*The Boxcar Children*, *The Babysitters Club*, the Christy Miller series, and Nancy Drew books by the dozens—and started picking up religious books, travelogues, and nonfiction works as my reading skills advanced.

In junior high school I happened to pick *A Wrinkle in Time* by Madeleine L'Engle off the school bookshelf. To say that moment changed my life forever would not be an exaggeration. I subsequently devoured all of Madeleine L'Engle's young adult fiction and started reading her spiritual memoirs as a high school student. Madeleine (I can refer to her by her first name. I wrote her a fan letter to which she responded, and from that point on she included me in her annual holiday letter; we were friends) was a Christian mystic. She opened my mind to an entirely different style of faith than I grew up with, for which I am eternally grateful. She was a practicing Episcopalian who easily blended spirituality with metaphysics and cellular biology. Unlike the faith of my youth, which reacted defensively to science and spent a lot of effort in combating the theory of evolution, Madeleine was not threatened by—and even found spiritual inspiration in—the sciences. She was more than okay with the unknown and said, "It does not matter that we cannot fathom this mystery. The only real problem comes when we think that we have."[5]

Madeleine taught me that it was okay to ask really hard questions and okay to never arrive at an answer. She made the mysterious sound sexy, not scary. After all, a God that could be fully understood by the puny human mind couldn't be that impressive of a god, right? She also had a theory of redemption and forgiveness that I had never encountered, which came to comfort me during that confusing experience in Australia: She believed that God had a plan to rescue and restore *all* of creation into the kingdom of God and that every creature would eventually return to the fold, including Satan himself. As she pointed out, what kind of loving God would let anyone suffer for all of eternity? Was God too weak to keep working on people after their short earthly lives expired? She believed literally that "neither death nor life . . . nor things present nor things to come . . . nor anything else in all creation, will be able to separate us from the love of God in Christ Jesus our Lord."[6]

That idea gave me hope and appealed to my sense of empathy and love. I began to believe in an "all roads lead to Rome" version of heaven. Although Jesus explicitly said, "I am the way, and the truth, and the life. No one comes to the Father except through me,"[7] I reasoned that Jesus was more than merely human. Jesus was somehow both 100% human and 100% God at the same time. The Bible talked about Jesus existing as the Word before all of creation was in existence, so Jesus had to be much more than his brief thirty-some years of life on earth spent as a Western Asian Jewish man. I started to believe that Jesus's Spirit must have a way of reaching folks who have never heard of his earthly person, especially considering that millions of people would have been born before he existed or lived on opposite ends of the globe and never heard of him.

At that point I still believed in the place of hell, but I wasn't sure that it was eternal. I thought it may be more like the Catholic's purgatory, or perhaps it was still the fiery hell I always envisioned, but God's Spirit was still at work there as a sort of escape hatch. I still primarily thought that Christianity was the correct religion but that somehow God would allow misguided folks in other religions into the fold, not holding it against them for getting God's name wrong. More cracks formed in my rigid understanding of all things spiritual.

A short story by Leo Tolstoy that I read in college nicely summarized this new way of thinking for me. In the story the Archangel Gabriel overhears God blessing a man and wonders who it could possibly be. Gabriel roams the

Earth looking for a wise, holy man and doesn't find anyone he deems worthy of God's blessing. The angel asks
God to reveal to him the man God has blessed. God tells
the angel to look for the temple where a man is praying.
Once he finds the man, the angel is shocked to discover
the man praying to an idol. A false god. In a huff, he
returns to heaven and demands to know how God could
do such a thing. And God says, "It's true, he doesn't understand me completely and is praying to an incomplete idea
of who I am, but his heart is in the right place, and I look
not at the mind for proper understanding, but at the
heart."[8]

The concept of God that I was given as a child—that
God is a loving Father who knows each hair on the heads
of all of his creation, who cares about tiny birds and flowers in the field, who wants peace to return to earth, and
who is so desperate for humanity to return his love that he
made a horrific sacrifice by sending himself/his son to live
and be murdered in a brutal way in order to make a bridge
for people to come to him—that loving God wouldn't pun-
ish people for being born in a part of the world where the
dominant religion isn't Christianity, right?

Was I really a Christian by choice, or was it simply
because I was born to Christian parents in the United
States? If I had been born in Iran or Indonesia, wouldn't I
probably be Muslim? If I had been born in Japan, wouldn't
I likely be Shinto? If born to an Aboriginal family in Australia, wouldn't I practice Tjukurrpa? If born in India, wouldn't
I be Hindu?

It didn't seem right, fair, or loving for one religion to have an exclusive grip on eternal paradise. I still identified as Christian after my time in Australia, even more so after being forged by fire all on my own without community support, but I started believing that Christians wouldn't be the only folks in heaven. Surely Jewish people were the first Chosen Ones and would be there—at least the Jewish people born before Jesus's life who didn't have the chance to accept or reject Jesus's message. The faithful Muslims I met must have a path to heaven too, even if it would be different than my "pray the prayer" experience.

After Australia, my faith became more mysterious and more inclusive. I felt comforted after reasoning out a way for millions of humans to avoid burning in hell for all eternity.

Nuance

THE NEXT SPIRITUAL CHALLENGE CAME during my junior year of college. I chose Marquette University—a Catholic, Jesuit university—because I was pre-physical therapy, and their physical therapy program was ranked twelfth in the nation at that point. Growing up, I had an ugly belief that Catholics weren't "real" Christians because (so I thought) they prayed to saints and worshiped Mary. Never mind that the Catholic church was the original Christian church and had been around for close to two thousand years before the Evangelical Free Church of America was born in 1950.[9] I was judgmental toward Catholics and didn't see many Catholic people, aside from one of my best childhood friends, taking their faith seriously in the way I measured faith. Being at Marquette exposed me to faithful, devout Catholic believers and was another small crack in my uptight, judgmental evangelical attitude.

In my junior year, my roommate and I befriended a man named Marc. Marc was obviously gay. I was fascinated. He was open and out while at a Christian school and did not seem bothered or held back by his sexuality. He was full of life, happy, and fun to hang out with. His huge smile lit up the room. Becoming friends with an openly gay man—who still professed to be a Christian no less—sent me reeling.

Although I don't remember any sermons against or explicitly renouncing homosexuality while growing up, the background vibe of my culture was certainly that it was a sinful choice and not compatible with Christianity. Whether from the exclusive teaching on heterosexual relationships or snarky jokes and mean put-downs of anything remotely gay (or even the use of *gay* as an insult), the point came across.

Other sins people may suffer from—jealousy, greed, selfishness—those are compulsions that come and go despite our best efforts to resist them. Being gay meant someone was daily choosing to live a life of sin, living contrary to God's plan for his people. They weren't even trying to live a blameless life if they were openly gay. At least, that was my ignorant view up until meeting my friend.

Sometime after meeting Marc and realizing that he genuinely believed in God and seemed to be quite naturally gay, I came across the wonderful documentary by Daniel Karslake called *For the Bible Tells Me So.* In the film, Karslake explores Christianity's approach to homosexuality and dives into biblical interpretations, the history of sexuality as a cultural issue, and the biology of sexuality as an innate orientation. The film examines some of the few passages of the Bible—especially the Sodom and Gomorrah story—that seem to condemn a homosexual lifestyle and offers context and a more accurate historical interpretation.

Karslake ripped the rug right out from under me.

The film's target audience is Christian parents with a gay child and follows four different families who took various approaches to their children's coming out. One set of

parents were offended, hurt, and opposed to it, shaming
their child and severing ties. Another set of parents kept a
"hate the sin, love the sinner" approach, which is equally, if
more subtly, hurtful and harmful. And two families were
genuinely supportive, becoming allies and activists alongside their children. The results of the different parenting
approaches were predictable and drastic. One child suc-
cumbed to suicide, another essentially cut her family off,
and the other two maintained healthy, loving connections
to their families of origin.

The most impactful part of the film for me was the seg-
ment when Karslake explains some of the biological under-
pinnings of sexual orientation. The movie talked about the
tendency for later-born boys to be gay, referring to the
mother's womb becoming "leaky" and feminizing the fetus
with her hormones more with each subsequent pregnancy.

The further research I did confirmed what I was learning. Homosexuality has both a genetic and cultural aspect
to it, like almost every other trait. Genetically there are
higher chances of being gay if another sibling in the family
is gay—a fourfold increase, in fact. Even more significantly,
half of the time one twin is gay, his identical twin brother is
also gay. DNA studies have firmly identified at least one
gene—with theories that more are present—partly responsible for a homosexual orientation.[10]

To think that God made people to be gay naturally
changed the game for me. How could it be sinful if it was a
person's perfectly natural state and not really a choice?
Which got me wondering how love—healthy, caring,

consensual, and respectful love—could ever be wrong? My heart pounded as I allowed myself to admit that I no longer believed that homosexuality as an orientation or homosexual behavior itself was sinful. I cringed, glancing up, waiting for the lightning bolt to strike, but the skies were silent.

I showed the film to the small group that I led at the time through Campus Crusade, and within a week, I was sat down for a stern talking-to by a younger, freshman boy attempting to rein me in from steering these poor, innocent girls in my group away from Christ. He had asked to meet me for coffee, which was strange since we had never hung out before. I had no idea what was coming until we sat down and he started in on his attack—I mean, concerns—claiming that I was abusing my position of leadership and presenting falsehoods to my group. "How dare you question the obvious biblical interpretation of the sinfulness of homosexuality?"

I stood my ground and suggested that he watch the documentary as he may have something to learn about biblical interpretation. He declined. The whole meeting was insulting, self-righteous, and maddening and did nothing to change my mind. It did contribute to my exit from the Campus Crusade group on campus, however.

The experience of something that I took to be God's honest truth *changing* was a pivotal moment for me. I felt quite shaken up. If I was somehow misled or the church was wrong in its attitude toward homosexuality, what else could I be wrong about?

How could the church be wrong?

The possibility that the Bible could be misinterpreted—or worse, intentionally twisted—to make it say what society wants it to say was crushing to think about. I trusted the Bible completely until then, but as I learned about the specific issue of homosexuality as it shows up in the Bible, I realized that something terrible had happened.

Not only is the concept of sexual orientation much newer than the Bible itself (it was identified and named in the mid-1800s),[11] but the word *homosexual* was not even a word when the Bible was written, not in English or in Hebrew, Greek, or Aramaic, the languages used to write the Bible. The seven measly biblical passages—26 total verses* out of the 31,102 verses of the Bible—that mention anything close to the idea of homosexuality are not discussing loving, committed relationships between equal partners. When understood through the context of the original cultures, they are discussing rape, gang rape, prostitution, and pedophilia, which I believe we can all agree are wrong behaviors.

At the time the New Testament was written, homosexual behavior was frowned upon because it was considered a sign that the man had poor self-control, unable to be satiated by women alone. Most homosexual interactions of that time were between an older man and a young protégé and were likely power- and control-driven, pedophiliac, and not consensual or ethical. Hardly the loving homosexual relationships we scrutinize today.[12]

---

* Genesis 9:20–27, Genesis 19:1–11, Leviticus 18:22, Leviticus 20:13, 1 Corinthians 6:9–10, 1 Timothy 1:10, and Romans 1:26–27.

While it may not be the dominant orientation, homosexuality is completely natural. I came across an article by *Yale Scientific* that states there are at least 450 observed animal species that exhibit homosexual behavior.[13] The author even outlines ways in which homosexuality has evolutionary advantages. The gays are good for the biological advancement of the human race! Hallelujah!

In addition to homosexuals, intersex and transgender animals are also observed in the animal kingdom. Google "intersex cardinal" for a striking image of a bird that is not fully male or female. I heard an interview of Frans de Waal on Sean Carroll's *Mindscape* podcast in which he discusses a transgender bonobo.[14] In childhood this anatomically female bonobo mimicked her father's behavior rather than her mother's, and as she aged, she spent most of her time socializing with the other males. She acted male, performing the typically male displays of aggression. de Waal surmised that, if he could directly ask her, she would likely identify as male. That was shocking for me to learn.

I could conceive of gender as a cultural phenomenon that humanity had created and changed over time. But to think that animals display signs of being biologically or hormonally (or culturally) transgender was amazing. It reinforced the idea that being queer is natural and normal, not something for which humans should be punished or abused.

Over the years I've kept digging into the issue, reading books like Matthew Vines's *God and the Gay Christian: The Biblical Case in Support of Same-Sex Relationships*. Vines holds the Bible in high regard, seeking to follow biblical mandates and instruction in his own life and in his writing and teaching. He painstakingly goes through the scriptures' discussion of the marriage covenant and tries to get at the root of what matters within a marriage. Having children does not seem to be the main requirement but rather commitment and fidelity. Vines demonstrates how a consensual, committed, monogamous homosexual relationship is not an affront to God's kingdom and is as equally honoring of the marriage covenant as a consensual, committed, monogamous heterosexual relationship.

I read *Becoming Nicole: The Transformation of an American Family* by Amy Ellis Nutt, a persuasive book on the science and biology behind transgender folks. It highlights one specific child in a family on her journey and struggle for acceptance. Nutt taught me about gender dysphoria and many of the various biological reasons a person may not identify with their outward appearance. Not only are some folks born with male and female genitalia whose parents are forced to pick one gender in which to raise them—which may not end up being how the child identifies later—but there are also genetic and hormonal alterations that can happen during development in the womb that would cause a person to identify as one gender while looking like another. Nicole's story—a transgender girl with a twin brother, a dubious father who took a while but eventually became her most vocal supporter and advocated for her rights, and an immediately supportive mother who only wanted her child to be happy—was a compelling read that completely changed my views on transgender issues.

Intersexion: A Story of Faith, Identity, and Authenticity by Cynthia Vacca Davis tells the story of a man named Danny who was born looking like a girl but internally knew that he was a boy as a toddler. As a three-year-old he told his mom that when he grew up, he would be a boy. When puberty hit, he dropped a testicle, grew a penis, developed breasts, and got his period! Reading this direct account of an intersex person was eye-opening, and witnessing his struggle to fit into his conservative Christian family and church life was crushing. He tried so hard to be the good Christian girl everyone wanted him to be, but it ultimately led to severe physical and mental health problems. Anytime I learn about a people group different from my own and get to know an actual person from that group, it is a transformative experience. This book made me feel like I had met Danny in real life.

All these things I was learning significantly changed the way I looked at my fellow humans, particularly those on the queer spectrum. My heart broke in realizing the horrors being committed today under the guise of allegiance to a loving god. *Judging* another person for being their true, authentic self now seemed far worse than having the bravery to honor one's true identity, no matter how countercultural. The more I learned in this arena, the more passionately affirming I became. After watching that documentary in college, I set out with evangelical fervor to convince fellow believers of our cultural misunderstanding and abuse of the Bible on this topic. Aside from preaching to anyone anytime I got a chance, I vocally supported legislative efforts for marriage equality. Over the years I began attending Pride parades (inviting my church community to join me), supporting The Trevor Project, and donating to Mama Bears and other organizations aimed at supporting this marginalized group of people.

It is more of a cultural offense to be queer than a moral affront. The people in the Bible weren't aware of sexual or gender identities, and the men writing the Bible were not asking those questions or concerned with that topic in the way we are today. Other people groups, by contrast, have had a richer understanding of both gender and sexuality when you look outside the white Western bubble.

Humans throughout cultures and times have fallen outside of cisheteronormativity, with societal attitudes toward queerness ranging wildly. Indigenous Americans recognize at least four gender groups, including two-spirit folks[15]; Indian society has Hijras[16]; Mexicans celebrate Muxe folks[17]; and baklâ people live in the Philippines.[18] These various people groups around the world commonly recognized a third gender that is neither male nor female and often revered it. Whitewashing and colonization have pushed all these people into the margins, but I learned that there have been societies around the world for thousands of years in which the concept of gender was more expansive and gender-bending was the norm and even honored.

REALIZING THAT CULTURE HEAVILY FACTORED into the writing of the Bible in ways we cannot now even perceive—and recognizing that we are far removed from those original cultures—made me look differently at the Bible. My views on the Bible had already been significantly affected by three semesters of required Theology coursework at Marquette. They added to this new, more complex, and better informed understanding of my religion's sacred text. In class we discussed the various councils—the First Council of Nicaea, the Council of Chalcedon, the First Council of Constantinople, and the like, in which human men—men who had never met Jesus—made monumental decisions defining aspects of the Christian faith that became bedrock. These men defined the concept of the Trinity and decided on behalf of the rest of us that Jesus was both 100% God and 100% man. The various church councils also decided which books to include (meaning that other books were considered and didn't make it) in the Bible.

I was shaken to realize that human men got to make such monumental decisions concerning the Bible and Christian dogma, and while I was sure that they spent time praying and discerning God's will, I couldn't help but wonder how much of their own humanness got in the way. I certainly never received a direct answer from God when I asked for guidance over any decision in my life. Did God communicate more clearly with these early Christian leaders? Or did they pray and make the best guess available to them and hope God directed their choices? I still trusted that God was in charge and guided those decisions, but I was certainly a bit rattled thinking that it all could have gone so differently.

The Bible no longer seemed like a clear, straightforward blueprint for living, an open path into God's own heart. Instead, it became a human experience, the product of flawed people struggling to understand this idea of God through their limited lenses. This new perspective made many of the violent, angry, tribal stories from the Hebrew portion of the Bible easier to stomach as I could write them off and say that those were never God's intended ways of being. I reasoned that the ancient Israelites made God into their own image (as we still do today), which at the time was tribal and war-like, and put their words into God's mouth. I figured that genocide, enslavement, and colonizing land that already belonged to others was humankind's way of life at the time, not God's desired plan for all of humanity. I decided that patriarchy was a flawed concept that came about after God's original design in the garden, and that God never intended for men to rule over women.

As I continued to wonder over and investigate my faith, I read a lot about the Bible itself. *How The Bible Actually* Works: *In Which I Explain How an Ancient, Ambiguous, and Diverse Book Leads Us to Wisdom Rather Than Answers—and Why That's Great News* by Pete Enns is a dive into ancient biblical thought-processes. According to Enns, the Israelites who wrote most of the Bible were not concerned with facts and historical accuracy in the way our culture is today. They were more interested in what the story had to say and focused on the overall message, even if they had to change some facts to make their point clear. *What Is the Bible?: How an Ancient Library of Poems,*

Letters and Stories Can Transform the Way You Think and Feel about Everything by Rob Bell goes deeper into the cultures of various biblical time periods, explaining how many familiar stories from the Bible would have sounded to the original audience. Often, that perspective significantly changes the meaning. *The Jesus I Never Knew* by Philip Yancey also explained how Jesus's Jewish culture and life under Roman occupation affected the nuance of his message. It focused primarily on Jesus's humanity—his emotions, reactions, gentle leadership, and countercultural ways. *The Universal Christ: How A Forgotten Reality Can Change Everything We See, Hope For, and Believe* by Richard Rohr was a mind-blowing book that explored the idea of Jesus as the "Christ figure" and how that concept is far larger than any one religion.

Jesus Feminist: An Invitation to Revisit the Bible's View of Women by Sarah Bessey focused on the patriarchal lens of the Bible and how the few verses and passages that seem to uphold a patriarchal view can be interpreted differently in a way that is much more honoring of women. She showed how Jesus interacted with the women around him and highlighted how supportive and affirming he was. She offered a different interpretation of the passages written by Paul that are frequently used by folks looking to silence and subjugate women. She also challenged my habit of referring to God by male pronouns and demonstrated several times throughout the Bible that God used female analogies to describe themselves, causing me to start trying to use she/her pronouns and ultimately landing on they/them pronouns for God.

Books about the Bible added depth and complexity to my understanding and gave me a more nuanced perspective when reading those ancient words.

A world full of blurred lines and shades of gray felt scary compared to the simplistic black-and-white views I'd held before. It was hard not to feel overwhelmed and in over my head since I didn't have the background understanding to make the original message of the Scriptures clear, and making things clear and rigid is comforting, as long as I'm on the right side of wrong. However, this is a developmentally childish way of thinking, a psychologically immature way of perceiving the world.[19] I found myself struggling to evolve along with this more expansive perspective. Couldn't I go back in time to when ignorance was bliss? No. I felt pulled along on this journey, getting slightly frightened of where it was taking me.

Now I had a harder time reading the Bible with all this cultural context added in. I didn't have time to study the norms and ways of life for Hebrew people in the thirteenth century BCE or of the Jewish people living under Roman occupation in the first century CE. I didn't have time to learn the original languages of the Bible, which could make certain passages of Scripture translate much differently. I could still take things at face value, but reading the Bible in English, reading only the books men picked to include while excluding other perspectives and voices, and reading it all through twenty-first century, white, American, middle-class eyes felt like reading the Bible via the longest game of "telephone" ever played.

How many times had the text I was looking at been orally passed along, eventually written down, picked over, and translated before making its way to my ears? How many statements would have shocked the original listeners yet felt blandly anticlimactic to me? I now knew that I was missing out on a lot of between-the-lines context that would have caused certain phrases or concepts to leap off the page in the eyes of the original audience. It felt scary, but more honest, to realize how complex and layered all this truly was. I became much more skeptical when people discussed what "the Bible clearly says." In fact, it had never felt less clear.

To return to the metaphor from my testimony, as I skated along this spiritual path, I began encountering hard, frozen blobs of ice stuck fast in my way. I wasn't sure what to do with them, so I decided to skate around them for the time being. The desire to simply *keep skating*, for life to remain simple and straightforward, black and white, was strong. But I couldn't help becoming acutely aware that the glassy, clean, easy path I had been skating on all these years wasn't as smooth as I thought.

Afterlife

THROUGHOUT THE REST OF MY college and post-grad years at Marquette, I maintained an open-minded, progressive approach to Christianity. I proudly supported the LGBTQ+ community. I became much more interested in volunteering and community services—influenced in no small part by those social-justice-minded Jesuits—and held a looser concept of salvation that was accessible to people of many faiths.

Somehow—I didn't spend too much time dwelling on it—I still thought God would judge some as worthy and some not. I guess by their hearts or approaches to life? I still identified as Christian, but I was more open to considering the wisdom of other religions. I read up on Zen Buddhism, and I enjoyed the poetry of Bashō and Ryōkan.

I joined Amnesty International on campus and worried about suffering around the globe, attending marches to get "Boots on the Ground!" in Darfur. I traveled with my school's University Ministry group to Belize and met JVIs (Jesuit Volunteers International) who were working to establish improved living conditions and rights for prisoners in Belize's jail system. I met local grassroots organizers—including a magnetic, larger-than-life woman named Perla—doing great things to help their own people. Perla had developed a program to improve poverty by giving families a cow, chickens, or a pig, teaching them how to best care for the animals, and then allowing them the choice to either eat, keep, or sell their animals a year later. Her program was so successful that she was flown around the world to present it to various organizations.

Learning about political situations around the world drew me into politics at home as well. Growing up, I was often trapped in the car on long road trips while my dad listened to Rush Limbaugh. I observed my parent's distain of the Clintons, and I absorbed the idea that Christians equal Republicans. I voted for Bush in the 2004 election without thinking much about it. As soon as I started paying attention to politics, I was drawn to the liberal side of things. I was quite taken with Barack Obama while I was still at Marquette, consuming *The Audacity of Hope* like it was the blueprint for a perfect society. I even went to hear him speak in person while he campaigned through Milwaukee during his 2008 presidential run.

After walking away from the (as I then saw them) close-minded, judgmental Campus Crusade crowd, I became involved in leadership at my local nondenominational church in Milwaukee. It was a young church, and I helped write up our mission statement concerning hospitality, which outlined how we wanted to be intentionally welcoming to newcomers. I oversaw the "greeters"—folks posted at the entrance to the church to notice and welcome any new faces—and I developed a system for new people to feel truly welcomed and connected. I attended The Global Leadership Summit put on by Willow Creek, a Chicago megachurch, along with the leadership board from my church, where I learned from Colin Powell and Bill Hybels (before his public downfall). I was still a deeply invested, earnest, devout believer.

I was so earnest that I worried that my life had been too easy. I'd had a charmed childhood (aside from my back issues, which I had long ago brushed off). My parents were still married and in love, I always had plenty of close friends, I was surrounded by fellow Christians wherever I went, and I was never persecuted or even teased for my faith. Never was I called to martyrdom or to sacrifice anything or anyone close to me as Abraham was with his son Isaac in the book of Genesis. I worried that God couldn't possibly know if I really loved them because I'd never had to prove it.

So, during my junior year of college, as everyone around me was turning twenty-one and taking over the bar scene downtown, I decided to "sacrifice" drinking for six months to prove my love for God and to prove that they meant more to me than my contemporaries' approval and being perceived as fun and cool.

Yes, I was still very much a Christian.

THE NEXT BIG SCHISM DIDN'T come for a while. I graduated from Marquette with my bachelor's degree in psychology and from their graduate physical therapy program a couple years later, then moved to Spokane, WA, with two of my friends from university. A few months later, I met my husband. We stayed up late talking about religion and politics and attempting to solve the mysteries of the universe. He was the first man I dated who loved to talk even more than I do, and I fell in love quickly.

After dating for a year, he proposed on the way home from a weekend trip over to Seattle. The weekend had not gone as he planned, and after several botched proposal attempts, he pulled off a random exit on I-90, put the still-running car in park at the side of the road, came around to my door and got down on one knee while I remained buckled in my seat, too shocked to move. We're eleven years into our marriage now, and we are still talking about the big stuff: hypocrisy in the church, the Religious Right, and the intersection of faith and politics.

My husband was more political than me, and I became much more interested and passionate about politics after talking with him for hours. He had paid attention to politics since he was a young boy. He'd thought evil had won when Bill Clinton was elected, but he slowly came to see the commandeering of the conservative Christian crowd by the Republican party and eventually swung to the left.

The exact moment eludes me, but at some point a few years into our marriage, we were talking about eternity (as one does), and I stopped and thought about hell for five whole minutes. As soon as I tried to truly conceive of eternity—millions and billions and trillions of years—hell was no longer a valid concept for me. Someone who lived a measly eighty-two years on planet Earth and never quite committed their soul to God was doomed to suffer horrific torture for *e-t-e-r-n-i-t-y*? No.

No.

Love couldn't do that. No possible way.

With my heart pounding once again, I dared to say aloud—and this time with my husband as my witness—that I no longer believed in hell. The skies were once again silent. I still wasn't struck down. I felt a bit scandalous—worried about these new opinions that I'd considered total heresy just a few years prior, but also thrilled at the realization that I could, in fact, change my mind on such a major issue. My husband had already come to the same conclusion, which gave me some comfort since I trusted his opinion as much as my own.

This felt major, much bigger than no longer believing homosexuality was a sin. Heaven and hell are part and parcel of Christianity. If hell wasn't real, then what about heaven? Outside of my conscious awareness, the beginning of doubt concerning God themselves began to grow. It didn't occur to me at that time to question the existence of God. I still needed the idea of God to be real. God was a balm to suffering. They provided me with a sense of relief knowing divine justice would eventually catch up to all the "bad guys." God provided my primary sense of purpose and value in this world. Instead of questioning God's existence, all I could manage was the mental gymnastics required to decide that hell was bad theology. I clung to my concept of a loving God, moving mountains of theological dogma to do so.

Some of the baggage I carry from my upbringing involves questioning the status quo. The attitude at my church, and later at the college ministry where I served, was that they had figured out all the correct answers. Faith components were black and white. They knew exactly what to believe, and any doubts or alternate opinions were flat-out wrong. It took me a long time to become comfortable with doubt because of my early religious culture.

The faith of my youth was rife with prejudice. I judged Catholics. *My* church didn't revere Mother Mary or pray to the saints, so that was clearly incorrect. I judged Pentecostals. *My* church didn't practice theatrical dancing in the aisles, laying on of hands for miraculous healing, or speaking in tongues, so that was obviously off-base. I judged Mormons. Why were they pretending to be Christian when they'd started a completely new religion? *Wrong.* I judged Christians who swore—not "talking the talk"! I judged Christians who drank (at least, until I started drinking at age eighteen). The Bible clearly condemns drunkenness. I judged Christians who didn't behave exactly as *I* thought they were supposed to behave. So for me to question something as basic and foundational as the afterlife felt incredibly intimidating.

Although the early influence of Madeleine L'Engle had laid some groundwork for me to question the mechanics of hell, it still felt quite heretical to stop thinking it existed altogether. However, I was comforted to find out that I was far from alone. Although I hadn't read it when it first came out, I remembered folks clutching their pearls over Rob Bell's *Love Wins: A Book About Heaven, Hell, and the Fate of Every Person Who Ever Lived*. I checked that out, and I was surprised to read in the opening statement that Bell wasn't saying anything new. It was practically a book report on previous versions of Christian thought and consensus on the afterlife, which varied wildly and with great debate. Christians have never been in 100% agreement about anything, but I didn't realize the number of other theories on the afterlife that have existed for thousands of years!

Bell showed how most of the early church believed that hell was a place of rescue and reconciliation, not of torture and punishment for eternity; the process of transformation in hell might be painful but ultimately led to forgiveness and reunion with God. God was believed to lovingly use "refining fires" to rehabilitate someone to ultimately allow them into God's presence. Bell refers to Martin Luther (famous for starting the Protestant Reformation) as saying, "God forbid that I should limit the time of acquiring faith to the present life. In the depth of the divine mercy there may be opportunity to win it in the future."

Bell pointed out several theological and moral problems with the concept of eternal suffering in hell. For example, the "age of accountability" concept that certain Christians believe—that innocent children who tragically die before the age of twelve will automatically go to heaven—raises a moral quandary. If it's true, and if eternity is a binary choice between heaven or hell, then shouldn't we kill any kids we care about before their twelfth birthday? Then they are guaranteed to go to heaven, and we don't risk letting them make the choice of rejecting God themselves to end up in hell for eternity. That sounds both loving in the eternal sense and horrific in the earthly here-and-now sense and is clearly not a moral decision sane people would make.

Bell posed this question: does God suddenly change character when a person dies, going from unconditionally loving and thirsty for reconciliation one moment to vicious and punitive the next? The very idea of hell would make it seem that God is able to be unloving and unconcerned once a soul has left Earth. As an alternative, Bell posited that perhaps because the very essence of God is supposed to be love—"love is from God, and whoever loves has been born of God and knows God. Anyone who does not love does not know God, because God is love"[20]—that choosing to reject that love *during your earthly lifespan* creates a present hell on Earth.

I was attracted to the idea of our earthly lives embodying the role of heaven or hell. I have circled the sun enough times at this point to realize that shit happens to everyone. Good and bad people all have both good and bad things happen in their lives, and suffering seems to be one of the few guarantees of the human experience.

While the suffering itself feels unfair, we have some control in our reactions to it. We can strive to be psychologically healthy—to process the grief and pain, to share our experience with our close circle and be bolstered up by those we love, and to move beyond the pain or at least on to a point of acceptance—or we can choose to wallow in misery, play the victim, see only our pain and not our moments of joy, reject help and comfort, and generally make our lives a sort of hell.

It made sense for our daily attitudes and choices to make our current lives heavenly or hellish. If I am jealous, petty, envious, and insecure, if I never take credit or blame for my own decisions, if I am too timid to ever put myself out there in my relationships or aspirations, if I choose to live a closed-off life without any vulnerability or true intimacy, if I never learn gratitude and contentment, I could be living in hell as we speak. In contrast, when I live authentically, generously, and humbly, when I go after my dreams and process my failures well, when I exercise vulnerability and step outside my comfort zone to make friends, when I seek help where it's needed, when I admit I've made mistakes and ask for forgiveness, when I am not too proud to depend on others, and when I practice mindfulness and contentment with my situation in life, my life can feel heavenly.

I still believed God existed in a way that reached beyond religion and connected with all of humanity. I hoped that God truly was Love itself and would not let anyone be lost for eternity. Maybe God's power really was strong enough to defeat death—not only Jesus's death, but everyone's. Maybe it was strong enough to conquer the division between God and *all* of God's creation either before *or* after earthly death. I liked this theory. It was comforting to think that no one would suffer endlessly. It gave me an avenue to continue believing God to be a loving Being, which I desperately wanted to believe. I started wondering about what other theories concerning the afterlife had to say.

I stumbled across a book by Catherine Wolff called *Beyond: How Humankind Thinks About Heaven.* This book offers a thorough account of how humans have thought about the afterlife since nearly the beginning of recorded civilization. It reads like a college textbook on the afterlife, meaning it was drier and less interesting than I expected it to be, and I think it would appeal to people without any faith as an anthropological study. There were, however, parts that stuck out to me, particularly when she discussed John Lubbock's five stages of the evolution of religion.

First, according to Lubbock (in Wolff's summary), it is theorized that early humans were atheistic. This made sense to me; after all, we don't conceive of animals as believing in gods, and early humans were animals (as we remain today, however highly evolved). Fetishism reportedly came next, a time when people believed gods to inhabit objects like trees or animals. In other words, the concept of a deity had arrived but remained localized to the immediate, physical world. After that came totemism, in which nature itself was full of good and evil spirits. Shamanism evolved next, which involved the gods living in another realm for the first time, a "spiritual world." The final phase was idolatry, or the fashioning of gods in human form. Immediately upon this development, religion and politics intermingled, and people believed that their pharaohs, caesars, and other such rulers were gods sent from above.

Seeing religious beliefs outlined in such an academic way made this tiny thought in the back of my mind grow larger. I was beginning to realize how man-made the whole "God thing" felt. I was reading Wolff's book alongside other scientific books on paleoanthropology and human evolution (which I cover more in the next chapter), which added together made me strongly question the objective truth of religion. Seeing this path of evolution regarding spiritual and religious beliefs threatened its essential truth in my mind, an opinion I was having a harder time blocking out. If humankind slowly stopped seeing gods in nature only to invent whole spiritual worlds and hierarchies, none of these beliefs seemed to represent fundamental truths, just evolutionary development. Cultures change, and apparently religion changes along with them; was there anything more to it than that? I started to wonder.

The most interesting part of Wolff's book was the discussion of near-death experiences, or NDEs. NDEs have been recorded among the religious, the atheistic, the agnostic, and even the suicidal. There seems to be a common set of experiences in NDEs across ages, cultures, and religions (or lack thereof) as well, although the actual experiences vary greatly. Accounts frequently mention a tunnel or white light or seeing a movie-like review of their lives. Others often report an out-of-body experience or interacting with a beloved person who had previously died. Typically there is an enveloping feeling of peace, love, or oneness with the universe.

Folks tend to come out of the experience changed people, becoming more compassionate and loving. They might leave unhealthy relationships or feel spiritually transformed. Law enforcement, military folks, and mafia members (really!) have changed careers after an NDE as they find they can no longer tolerate living alongside such violence after feeling intrinsically connected to all humankind. Most folks become less religious as their experiences do not line up with what they were taught to expect about the afterlife, but they feel more spiritually alive than ever before. There were accounts from some folks who felt dread and horror during their NDEs, but that experience was thankfully rare. The horror wasn't from seeing a lake of fire, either, but rather because the tunnel of white light or the life review felt scary.

NDEs are a sticking point against my current philosophy eschewing the afterlife, and I will wrestle with this more in an upcoming chapter. Still, it is comforting to note that whether Muslim, Hindu, Christian, nonreligious, or atheistic—people who survive NDEs all experience eerily similar things, things that are overwhelmingly positive and peaceful, without judgment or condemnation. If there *is* something beyond this world, it does appear to be welcoming for everyone.

I was delighted to discover a television show that took up the topic of the afterlife in an engaging, humorous way. As a longtime fan of Kristen Bell, I was excited for the debut of Michael Schur's television show *The Good Place*. Bell stars in the leading role as the show tackles philosophical debates in a charming, highly entertaining manner. I enjoyed how the show handled the concept of a heavenly afterlife of eternal bliss. (Spoiler alert for what follows if you haven't seen the show!) Over the course of the series, a group of humans ends up traveling through different levels of the afterlife and struggling for eons to reach "The Good Place." They finally arrive only to discover that the souls who preceded them have turned into mindless pleasure zombies, no longer able to enjoy a literal eternity of perfection and bliss since everything has lost its meaning. Existence without an end felt pointless. In the last of an epic array of plot twists, the protagonists discover that heaven itself gets old after a while. They ultimately find a solution by offering a way out: a door into nonexistence, a truly final end that renders the afterlife meaningful once more.

As a young Christian, I remember feeling guilty for worrying about heaven, because I always found myself restless and bored during prolonged worship in church. I was taught that in heaven we would live in mansions and walk streets of gold but also sing "hallelujah" to God for eons on end. What child (or adult, for that matter) wouldn't be concerned that an eternity of singing God's praises would become unbearably boring? Setting aside the idea that hell might not be real, how could an eternity of anything in heaven be endlessly satisfying and enjoyable?

Knowing that human beings with free will inevitably make unhealthy choices, I had to wonder if we would no longer have free will in heaven. Did we get there and turn into God's puppets? Would we no longer be individuals with a personal will at all? And how does heaven *work*, specifically? Where is it? Another dimension? A multiverse? An immaterial state of being in which our individual selves meld into the being of God? My list of questions was growing, and I had nothing close to an answer.

This whole time I had kept skating along over my reworked and redefined Christian faith, confident that the ice would hold. However, once I no longer believed Christians have an exclusive grip on salvation or that heaven and hell are anything remotely like what I was taught growing up, a fine network of cracks appeared in the ice beneath my feet.

Creation

ALL THROUGHOUT HIGH SCHOOL, I had self-righteously covered my ears whenever evolution came up in class. My kindergarten through eighth grade years had been spent at a private Christian school, saving me from learning blasphemy at a young age. But at my public high school, I was exposed for the first time to historical and scientific teaching that took evolution as fact.

My anthropology class made me viscerally uncomfortable, amplified by my clearly liberal teacher, Mr. O'Conner, and his eagerness to debate with students. I struggled with wanting to learn but feeling spiritually attacked in his class. He taught us things that I *knew* to be false, namely that the Earth and humankind had been formed gradually over millions of years. My pulse pounded in my ears and my breath quickened in his class as I wrestled with the tension of wanting to be a martyr and boldly defend my faith against this heathen teacher versus being the good, straight-A student I was expected to be.

I fled to another history teacher at my high school who attended the same church as me, and I asked him for guidance and ammunition. We sat down over a study hall period while he went over the "evidence" for creationism with me, including photos of fossil footprints of dinosaurs in the same timeline as human footprints (which, it turns out, isn't accurate information).[21] I was comforted but did not feel bold enough to directly confront Mr. O'Conner with the truth. Instead, I paid selective attention in his class, and even until quite recently, I maintained a scant understanding of human evolution. Over the years, my views on biblical inerrancy changed, and I became curious to fill in my gaps of knowledge.

While I was on the never-ending hunt for content to market the physical therapy clinic I operated in 2020, a book called *First Steps: How Upright Walking Made Us Human* by Jeremy DeSilva jumped out at me. The book attempts to answer the question of when and why our ancestors first started walking. The author is a paleoanthropologist and dives deep into early human and prehuman history, looking at all kinds of fossils and evidence of our origins.

DeSilva's book was absolutely fascinating for me to read. Sometime during college I had come to accept the scientific truth of the theory of evolution. At that point I thought evolution and Christianity were in fact compatible, that God could have written the laws of the universe—thermodynamics, gravity, etc.—and set off the Big Bang themselves. Yet I had never filled in my gaps of knowledge on the topic. As I read *First Steps*, my mind reeled while I began to question for the first time whether God had ever been involved in the formation of the universe.

Within Christianity there is the belief that God made humanity to be the pinnacle of creation. All the plants and other animals came first, and humans were the crown—the *pièce de résistance*, perfectly and wonderfully made. So as I learned about the long path of human evolution from DeSilva, I wondered why our skeletons showed evidence of trial and error. Why do we have body parts that we don't use anymore, like wisdom teeth and the coccyx bone? DeSilva also showed me that the human foot is a convoluted thing that has changed and adapted over time to meet the differing needs of early hominins. Our ancestors' feet were better geared for gripping tree branches as we used to primarily live in trees for safety. Now our feet are both pliable and able to lock into a solid arch for support so that we can meld them onto the ground as we step down and lift our entire body weight up off the ground propelling us forward. As remarkable as that is, our feet are not the best possible design for a bipedal creature. The leftover pliability from needing to climb trees sets us up for injuries now. I see the evidence of this imperfect human design in my job: patients frequently come in for ankle sprains, shin splints, and plantar fasciitis because of vulnerabilities built into our feet. The ostrich foot is much better suited to walking efficiently on two legs and essentially is the design orthotists model prosthetic feet after. How could God intentionally shape us out of the clay in such a slapdash, wonky, imperfect way when a better way was possible?

An example often used in Intelligent Design rhetoric (an evangelical Christian theory designed to counter evolution) is the Watchmaker Analogy. William Paley used the analogy of stumbling across a watch on the ground: anyone would assume that the watch had been, at some point, designed by intelligent hands and dropped there, not that it could have spontaneously assembled itself over any length of time.[22] The argument claims that the universe and all it entails is far too complex and complicated to have come about through the long, drawn-out, trial-and-error process of evolution.

Convinced by that argument for a while, I was surprised to learn that the human eyeball—one of the most complex parts of the entire body, far more sophisticated than a watch—is not only imperfect (we have a blind spot where the optic nerve connects) but also isn't the only exquisitely made eyeball in creation. The octopus has a complex eyeball that is constructed better than ours. Not only is it extremely similar, utilizing rods and cones, but it lacks the blind spot because the optic nerve attaches differently.[23]

Why would God create a perfect eyeball for the octopus and not for us? Either God purposely designed our flawed eyeballs, or evolution takes a long, twisty path, pushed along by random mutations and decided by survivability that, over millions of years, comes up with interesting abilities and helpful adaptations for creatures. Apparently the process of evolution twice came up with the ingenious architecture of this kind of eyeball and did the best job of it with the octopus.

I cannot wrap my mind around how long one billion years is, or even one million. Our minds are not good at understanding such large numbers. I once heard Neil deGrasse Tyson say that the naked eye looking up at the night sky on a moonless evening can only see a few thousands stars.[24] All those sparkly stars add up to a measly few thousand! It is impossible to imagine all the stars we can see multiplied by 250,000 to reach 1 billion, and the universe is 13.7 billion years old, give or take a few years. That is incomprehensible—and would provide an awful lot of time for mutations, trial-and-error, and survival-of-the-fittest to do their things.

To put this all in perspective, consider that *homo sapiens* showed up on the scene around 300,000 years ago, giving hominins about 6 million years to slowly develop into what we are today, as DeSilva showed me. That is a lot of time to develop our current sophisticated design, and there were many previous versions of other human species that are now extinct. Our family tree has a lot of dead ends. I had never realized this, and the thought of human-like but not exactly human creatures rocked my world. I began to wonder—

Did Neanderthals go to heaven?

What about *Australopithecus sediba*, *homo habilis*, *homo naledi*, *homo erectus*, *homo heidelbergensis*—are they all in heaven too? Or did God only start to care when *homo sapiens* came on the scene? Intrigued by the book I read, my husband read another book about fossils and our late-night talks were filled with discussions of evolution.

From my perspective, it was looking like an intelligent, all-knowing Creator of any sort was not a required character to explain the existence of the natural universe. Once the materials were let loose at the Big Bang (and we still have no idea why or how or even if that exactly happened—mysteries abound), the laws of nature determined what happened next, and slowly, over billions and billions and billions of years, matter made its clumsy and convoluted approach to evolve into the Milky Way, planet Earth, moss and megalosaurs, insects and irises, blue whales and banyan trees, hydrangeas and hippopotamuses, and, eventually, human beings. As unbelievable as it is that *anything* exists, it throws an even more complicated wrench into the puzzle to fathom how something so complex as God could be formed prior to the rest of the universe.

Science has allowed us to develop a solid understanding of *how* all this came to be. Science cannot tell us *why* any of this is here. That is not the goal of science; religion and philosophy deal with the *why*. Science only attempts to understand and explain the known universe, and science has done a great job so far of studying our early origins as a species, as a planet, as a cosmos. Scientists do not have an unknown "x," a gap of knowledge, within our current understanding in which a godlike being is required to explain the way things are.

While it is a perfectly natural, healthy tendency to force meaning onto the chaos of our lives, the fact that God—in all the many forms God has taken over the millennia—is a universal human concept was no longer a compelling reason for me to believe in God as a fundamental, elemental reality. It seemed, rather, that groups of humans the world over had each made up their own version of a Higher Being because humans crave meaning and purpose, not because this Higher Being is actually out there.

With a lot of extra time to read and think after getting laid off at the beginning of the pandemic, I allowed myself to consider the basic existence of God, not yet taking the complete plunge into atheism, but dipping in a toe or two and finding the water to be warm. My husband, who shared many of the same doubts and critiques as I did but was not interested in doubting God's very existence, became nervous about my level of doubt. He downplayed his concerns, reasoning that I was in a depressed phase after getting laid off, becoming a stay-at-home mom against my will, and watching the world burn. He hoped I would come back around, and we skirted the topic of God for a while in our conversations.

ALTHOUGH I WAS BEGINNING TO truly wonder if God was real, I maintained an interest in all things spiritual. I started reading books from other faith traditions and was fascinated to learn about creation stories from various cultures. Humans have tried to answer the question "Why are we here?" in varied creative ways since we've been around. I love the Oneida creation story of Sky Woman coming down to our world, which was only water at that point. Geese saw her descending and rushed together to make a raft on which she could land. Other animals gathered and problem-solved, and Turtle provided his back for her to stand upon. The animals set about to bring up earth for her. One by one they dove down into the water, trying to bring up rich mud from the sea floor, but none could dive deep enough. Finally, Muskrat tried, and in a tragically selfless act, kept diving past the point of no return. His lifeless little body floated back up to the surface, and mourning turned to rejoicing when the others saw that Muskrat had clutched a bit of earth in his paws before giving his body as a gift to Sky Woman. They were able to use that earth to make Turtle Island, present day North and Central America.[25]

I thought this story full of community, collaboration, and self-sacrifice for the greater good was beautiful. Muskrats are now a beloved creature in my household. I have been humbled and inspired while learning about indigenous beliefs and attitudes toward creation and community from Robin Wall Kimmerer in *Braiding Sweetgrass*. In her book, she shared that Native peoples on Turtle Island were humble with regard to the Earth, knowing that plants and animals arrived first and humans are the "little brothers and sisters" of creation—here to learn from their elders. Indigenous people used sustainable practices like the honorable harvest, living in a reciprocal relationship with the natural world and cultivating gratitude and stewardship in their everyday actions. I can only imagine and grieve for how much healthier our planet might have been had Europeans not arrived with the delusion of Manifest Destiny, greed, and malice. If only.

I also learned about other cultures' creation stories that were bloody and violent, a testament to the way those societies viewed the world. The Babylonian creation story—the Enuma Elish, possibly the oldest creation story known—is a bloody, gory battle between the gods, with the Earth created out of the broken corpse of the goddess Tiamat.[26] At least the Hebrews' god started off creating the world in peace and declared it good! I saw our religious beliefs as myths and reflections of how we view ourselves and our roles in this world.

I began to question my innate desire for meaning and purpose, wondering if just because I needed something to be meaningful truly made it so. Various cultures had drastically different approaches to spirituality, making the gods into what they needed or wanted them to be through powerful psychological drives. Humans hear voices in static, see messages in tea leaves, and mine our dreams for guidance and direction. Just like little children thrive with structure and a predictable routine, fully grown humans also crave order and meaning. The idea of life being completely random is not comforting. Thinking that we are simply here for no real purpose and that no god above is watching or caring doesn't feel nice.

It rattled me to consider that the universe could have arisen slowly from nothing with no Creator pulling the strings. Seeing spirituality through a human-made, mythological lens shook me up even further and made me start to seriously consider the reality of God. After changing my beliefs in some major ways throughout my twenties, I had still never doubted the existence of God. I had doubted Christianity's exclusive ownership of God, had doubted the views of heaven and hell I'd been taught, had doubted many of the specific beliefs my flavor of religion touted—but never God itself. I felt a growing nervousness in my chest as a world where God was a human construct became a valid option. The reality of God began to shimmer and shift.

Ominous booms and groans from the ice cracking beneath my feet rang out. And yet, despite the dire appearance of my situation and my rattled nerves, I felt compelled onward in my search for ultimate truth, even if that meant leaving God behind. I couldn't continue dedicating my life and directing my every belief and action based upon an idea that may not be true. I needed to know if God was real or not.

Bias

THESE BIG QUESTIONS WERE ROLLING around in my head on a regular basis now. It was the spring of 2020, everything was shut down, I had been laid off, and my husband was working from home, so while the kids napped, I got the chance to go on long walks in my neighborhood. I would walk and wonder about God. As I questioned my lifelong beliefs, I remembered learning about the brain and the ways we think while I was back in college.

The human brain has long fascinated me. Between my undergrad psychology courses and the graduate-level neuroanatomy and neuropathology courses I took in my program, I learned a lot about the brain. A theory I had learned back then came to mind when I asked myself these tough questions about God: confirmation bias, our tendency to seek out information to fit what we already believe. It turns out humans have a strong compulsion to force new information to fit with what we already believe rather than being objective, quizzical, and open to changing our beliefs. We don't ever want to admit that we were wrong or made a bad choice, so we take any information that damages our viewpoints and rationalize it away, much like I did while fighting against evolution in high school: I purposely sought out information that would fit what I wanted to believe while ignoring information contrary to what I wanted to hear.

Humans ignore or reframe information that doesn't fit our worldview in a way that is beyond our conscious awareness. Imagine someone you dislike doing something considerate or kind for you. You might assume that they had a selfish reason or ulterior motive for acting that way before you believe that they are capable of general kindness. Or you may barely notice their kindness while your brain latches on to every instance of them behaving rudely or selfishly to maintain cognitive harmony with your negative opinion of their character. In contrast, a beloved friend who disappoints you will likely get a pass while you rationalize that they might be having a hard day but are certainly not a bad person.

On a grander scale, if you are a person who is worried about the climate (as I am) and want human societies to do more to curb our carbon emissions, you might latch onto every news story about adverse weather events and believe that we have serious work to do to avoid certain doom (as I do). If you are someone who believes that the planet constantly cycles through warming and cooling periods and that human beings aren't overly responsible for current changes in the environment, you might ignore certain stories and point out a cooler-than-average season as evidence against global warming. We routinely massage facts to make them say what we want them to say.

Had I been massaging the facts of reality to force God into the picture? Learning about God and dedicating my life to God, then seeing God's hand at work in my life: was it reality or Confirmation Bias 101?

When I questioned the reality of God, I thought about "hindsight bias"—our tendency to act like we knew things would turn out the way they did in retrospect. If you invest in a risky stock and it ends up performing well, you might turn around and explain that you had a gut feeling that it was a good idea to invest in that particular stock. However, if the stock went sideways, you'd likely chalk it up to bad luck and not a bad judgment call on your behalf.

Whenever I got a raise or a relationship that had been on the rocks suddenly improved, I would typically think that my prayers paid off and God had blessed me (even though it was not God's fault if the raise never came along). Similarly, we always see the winning sports team pointing up and thanking God after the game, but not the losing team's players blaming God for their loss. We praise God if we get all green lights while running late to work but don't think God is involved at all when we hit the normal number of reds and greens. Being religious and believing that God played an active role in the world, it was easy for me to assign credit to God after good things happened and to explain away negative events as one-offs or bad luck. I could look back in time at what had objectively, factually happened and only then decide what that meant.

For example, when I moved to Spokane after graduate school, I quickly joined an online dating website. I wasn't in a big rush to meet anyone, but a friend of mine was trying to get me to sign up, and I figured, "Why not?" It was free.

Within an hour of uploading my profile, I was contacted by a local man. As I perused his profile, I saw that he attended a nearby church and even led a small group (a major turn-on for my little Christian self). He seemed interesting and charming enough in our chats, so we set up a coffee date. That man turned out to be my husband. Looking back, to me it felt like destiny, that God brought us together through the wide world of online dating shortly after I moved and became open to meeting someone. Meanwhile, from his perspective, he had been out of college for years with a history of several failed relationships and online dating profiles that went ignored for months. He was aimlessly waiting for years for me to show up. He likes to joke that I was his mail-order bride flown in from the exotic Midwest. Hardly the romantic story of fate that I experienced. As my experience goes to show, we *want* to see greater meaning and purpose even when it does not exist. The brain will force facts to fit these subconscious motivations of ours without us even realizing that we are deluding ourselves.

Many of these mental shortcuts and biases make the world easier to understand. The environment we live in is large and complex, and the behavior of other people is hard to predict and even harder to control. Our brain is always striving for maximum efficiency, never wasting energy where it isn't crucial to do so. We rely on shortcuts and schemas to give our brains a break, but these are not always accurate. We tend to think of our brains as these supercomputers that control our every thought and function and that objectively take in data through which we can understand the world.

Unfortunately, our brains are as human as the rest of us. They fall victim to faulty logic and make mistakes.

I remember sharing a Facebook post during the 2012 election cycle, a photo of one of Mitt Romney's campaign hats with a "Made in China" tag sewn into the lining. I said something snarky criticizing Romney for talking big about American jobs while outsourcing his own campaign merchandise. I was rooting for Obama, so Romney was "the bad guy," and I found a post knocking him down that I immediately shared without much thought. And I was taken to town by a friend of a friend commenting that this was a fabricated image and that my rhetoric was fueling animosity and ill-will with no grace for the other or commitment to fact-checking.

I was mortified. I frantically checked Snopes and was horrified to find that I had shared a doctored image. I had been lured in by seeing what I wanted to see and blindly followed along. My brain had been tricked. I fell victim to faulty logic and made a mistake.

The brain's gullibility became clearer to me the more I learned about chronic pain from my profession. The bulk of my career thus far has been spent in the outpatient orthopedic world. Most of the time, my patients come in for pain of one type or another: back pain, knee pain, ankle sprains, torn ligaments, inflamed tendons—I've spent the last twelve years treating pain. Acute pain directly resulting from a tissue injury in a well-established time frame is easy enough to treat. Chronic or persistent pain, however, is an entirely different monster.

Pain is the alarm system of our body, warning us of danger; it is the only means our brain has of communicating this warning to us. Imagine that you put your hand too close to the hot stove. Your temperature-sensing nerves send a signal to the brain, and the brain recognizes the threat and causes you to feel pain so that you'll move your hand. Threat managed—the pain goes away.

Persistent pain happens when the brain can't get out of "threat" mode for any reason. Perhaps the original source of pain was traumatic due to abuse or a serious accident, or maybe you were raised with parents who freaked out over every little scratch, or your personal or cultural belief may be that all pain is disastrous and a sign of something seriously wrong. In persistent pain, your brain can latch onto pain like a bad song getting stuck in your head. That song distracts you and can stop other parts of the brain from working properly, affecting your physical being as well as your emotional and mental health, your sleep, your concentration, and even entire systems like the immune system or reproductive system![27]

An old assumption initially proposed by René Descartes over 400 years ago that lingers in the medical world to this day is that tissue damage—a torn muscle, frayed tendon, arthritic joint, or bulging disc—directly causes pain and that the amount of damage determines how severe the pain would be. This is simply not the case as proven again and again through research. Researchers have taken MRIs of people who are not complaining of shoulder pain and have found that one out of three people over the age of thirty has rotator cuff damage and no pain to show for it. Over the age of seventy that number goes up to two out of three people with rotator cuff tears who have no pain. There are similar statistics for neck and back arthritis, hip joints, knee joints, and bulging discs. There are people in this world walking around with bone-on-bone arthritis in their knees and absolutely no knee pain.[28]

I can certainly attest to this anecdotally from what I've witnessed at work. I am usually able to review my patients' medical charts, including any imaging reports, before seeing them for their initial evaluation. Countless times there has been a patient I'd review and begin to dread treating because their imaging reports were so nasty. People whom I expected to hobble in grimacing and groaning would come strolling up to my clinic with only mild complaints and get resolution quickly with treatment. Others whom I incorrectly assumed would be a breeze to treat since their reports looked mild or completely normal would turn out to have intractable pain that remained debilitating despite all my best attempts to alleviate it.

What we have learned in modern times through studying the body and the brain is that torn, bruised, or broken tissues do not directly *produce* pain. Rather, the body simply sends data to the brain for the brain to process. The data itself is neutral. Our brains take it in and decide what value to assign it depending on a wide variety of factors. It works the same way with all our senses. Our eyeballs don't do the seeing; they send visual information to the brain where it gets processed, and our brains can be tricked, as optical illusions demonstrate so well. Likewise, our ears don't themselves hear but rather send sound waves to the brain for interpretation. Our brain can be tricked here as well as demonstrated by auditory illusions. There are neat videos on YouTube that demonstrate these illusions if you're curious, or you can watch the entertaining National Geographic show *Brain Games*.[29]

There are two true stories we tell in the pain world, both dealing with nail injuries. In one story, a builder accidentally jumps down from scaffolding and onto a protruding nail, which punches through his work boot. Screaming in pain, he's taken by ambulance to the hospital and given pain killers along the way. Once at the hospital, providers rush to cut his boot off to assess the damage and are shocked to discover that the nail went cleanly between his toes, not a scratch to be found. The pain he truly and honestly felt was all produced by his brain as no physical injury had occurred.[30] He felt actual pain in his foot because his brain had watched a nail drive through his shoe and assumed that his foot had been injured, but there never was any tissue damage to the foot.

The other nail story involves a nail gun going off near a man's head. He couldn't see where the nail went. Undisturbed, he kept working and finished out the day. His fiancé cleaned a cut on his forehead that evening and thought nothing of it. The next day, he complained to his fiancé about being nauseous all day. She encouraged him to get it checked out, and eventually a scan showed that a nail had gone into his brain! He had a real, physical injury—to his head, no less—and did not feel any pain in the moment since his brain hadn't seen it happen.[31]

The brain is not as objective and accurate as we would like to believe, even when it comes to the physical sensations it causes us to feel in our bodies. The brain is influenced by context, past experiences, our culture, our mood, and a wide variety of factors at any given moment. I would go so far as to say that our brains—even among the most intelligent and objective of us—are gullible.

Knowing how gullible my own brain was, how prone to shortcuts and biases that may or may not reflect reality, I wondered how much of my faith made real sense and how much I simply *wanted* it to make sense. Did I see everything through God-colored glasses only because that was how I was raised and how my brain was trained to interpret the world? My brain might have been convinced of the presence of a loving, all-knowing Higher Being, but that didn't seem to be a good indicator of objective reality.

I was scared to truly question the existence of God. Most of my closest friends are progressive Christians who are also critical of literal readings of the Bible, believe in science, and affirm all people's identities, but they don't seem to have the same issue I had regarding the whole big picture. My husband was on the same page as me up until the point when I questioned God's existence. Was I being led astray? Was I off-base? Was I the only one feeling this way?

Talking over the dull roar of our kids playing or late at night while lying in bed, my husband and I reasoned through this together. While we shared many of the same thoughts and opinions, he was not as quick to question the literal existence of God as I was. He was equally critical of the church, equally appreciative of the cultural context and nuance needed to get a fair reading of the Bible, equally convinced by the facts of science, but he found he was still able to believe in an adjusted idea of God. He admitted that he almost doesn't care if God is real or not, but he appreciates having God to believe in to govern and order his life.

I could appreciate that. Maybe God was as real as traffic laws—not a fundamental part of the universe but necessary just the same. I know I am unusual in how much I think about all this, and certainly not everyone else cares this much. But I have always valued authenticity and genuineness above all else, so I needed to know if God was an actual, real thing or not. I needed to know that there was a bedrock truth to the existence of God to be able to keep believing.

I found that the more I learned—about biology, psychology, paleoanthropology, church history, the brain, the Bible—the more it caused a new picture to form in my mind, a picture that did not include a Divine Creator. My questions and doubts were leading me down to the most foundational beliefs a person can have. I felt truly nervous now, knowing that I was heading toward what felt more and more like an inevitable leap that would take me far away from the culture and worldview of my family and friends.

An inky stain was spreading across the ice where water had begun to permeate through the cracks. A point of no return was approaching.

Miracles

My attention was captured by the story of a random family on Instagram one day. A friend of a friend had a daughter who was in a freak accident, hitting her head and suffering massive brain damage. She was from a Christian family, and her dad worked in a pastoral role at a large church, so soon they had tens of thousands of people praying for a miraculous healing. The girl's father was *so certain* that a miracle was coming their way. They were praying and fasting, demonstrating faith that moves mountains while they boldly and expectantly asked God for a miracle. At one point the father even predicted the day they would receive said miracle, when his daughter would wake up from her coma and return to her sweet, bubbly self. As I watched from afar, unconnected and detached from the situation, my preemptive pain for this family twisted my gut.

To both no large surprise and terrible disappointment, the predicted day came and went with no extraordinary healing. Years later, the girl is still alive but drastically changed: nonverbal, immobile, and passively pushed around in a wheelchair. Her parents remain hopeful and have been impressively open and honest about their dark moments, showing a deep vulnerability to their online communities, leaning on their belief in God's ultimate wisdom and the idea that God works in mysterious ways.

Miracles are a tough issue for me to handle. I don't understand them on many levels. I don't understand the practicality of it—*how* does God intervene in the material world? Does God manipulate the laws of nature at will? I thought we were all supposed to have free will without divine control. Does the Spirit of God temporarily become physical in some mysterious way and perform invisible surgeries, change a person's biochemistry to stop their addiction or severe mental health disorders, or somehow lift someone out of poverty or abuse?

Aside from the *how*, far more upsetting to me was the *why*. Why do some people seem to receive miraculous healings and blessings and others—who are just as faithful, if not more so—suffer and even die prematurely? How does God choose? How hard we pray or how many people petition on our behalf doesn't seem to make a difference. Is it merit based? But I thought salvation and grace were free for all—are we secretly supposed to be collecting good points for the day we may need a miracle? Or is it totally random? That seems rather cold and heartless.

In my own faithful youth, I prayed and prayed and prayed for a miracle for my back. Even after I had surgery, I desperately wanted my curves to straighten, to smooth out my accordion-smooshed torso and gain several inches of height that I felt I was owed. I tried every route to a miraculous healing that I could think of: straight up asking God, bargaining with God, visualizing the healing, picturing waking up and noticing my shirts had all become midriffs, confidently speaking—out loud—that I knew God could do it if he felt like it, thinking I was all sly and reverse-psychologizing my Divine Lord and Maker. No luck. My torso remains short and smooshed, my spine wrapped in metal.

Mysterious things do happen, things that are not easy to explain. I know someone who worked in Ethiopia in the 1960s as a physician and met a young boy who seemed to truly think he was a dog. He crawled on all fours—with thick callouses on his knees to show for it—barked and growled and never spoke in his mother tongue. When his parents brought this boy to the doctor to be looked at, the doctor—who was a Christian—was at a total loss. He asked the family if they minded if he tried something unconventional. He crouched down low to the boy and in a sharp voice suddenly commanded the *demon* to leave the child's body in the name of Jesus. And the boy stood up and walked.

Miracle? Exorcism? Or was the psychological power of a commanding white man enough to bypass whatever mental coping strategy or plea for attention this boy was using and shock him back to "normal"?

Our minds are incredibly powerful. We've seen how easily our brains can be manipulated and tricked into seeing, hearing, feeling, and believing things that are not objectively true. If our brains think a person (or a prayer, a pill, a diet, or a specific treatment) is capable of a miraculous healing, our brains seem capable of making it so. That's the basic concept behind the placebo effect: a person takes a sugar pill that they believe will cure them, and they are cured, even if the pill did absolutely nothing.

With hindsight, we can assign blame or praise as we see fit. If the healing occurred and the miracle seemed to happen, "Praise be to God!" If it didn't work out, well then, "It's not up to us to know God's mysterious ways." Excuses or alternate explanations get God off the hook when things don't work out, often to the detriment of the miracle-less person. Maybe their faith wasn't strong enough, or God was using this to fix a flaw in their character, or worse. It's easy to say God comes through and prayers are answered when it works out as we want it to, but when it doesn't, what does that say about God? Should God only get the credit when things go in our favor and not when they don't? Isn't that a little unfair?

I was curious to know how rare miracles truly are and picked up a book called *The Improbability Principle: Why Coincidences, Miracles, and Rare Events Happen Every Day* by David Hand. It goes through just how possible "impossible" events really are. A lot of it comes down to math.

Say someone is diagnosed with an aggressive cancer, with a 1 in 500,000 chance of surviving. Well, that number is an actual possibility. There were 18.1 million people with cancer in 2020.[32] Eventually there will be over 500,000 cases of their type of cancer, and that 1 in 500,000 chance will happen for at least one person. Given enough opportunities—which, with eight billion people alive today, is easy—even miraculous healings are nearly guaranteed at some point. On average the odds are low, but that one specific person may be the one-in-a-million winner. While miraculous healings seem otherworldly, there are odds and probabilities at play that make miracles almost expected at least some of the time. Realizing this was more evidence for my growing conviction of a godless world.

Last summer I enjoyed a weekend at the lake with my close friends, and we were doing yoga on the deck on Sunday morning. We were outside, facing a small forest of trees through which the lake was peeking, soaking in the morning sun while we stretched and moved our bodies. I have always felt the most spiritually alive outdoors, so I was having a moment feeling *at one* with the trees and the birds already, when the instructor—telling us to check our grounding and stability—said, "Imagine if a big, big gust of wind were to come through magically" *right* when a gusty wind picked up and blew in our faces! The coincidence was uncanny, and we laughed out loud at the magic of it all.

Saying that miracles and unbelievable coincidences are not that unique, that math explains how these things can and even should be happening with regularity, doesn't take away the wonder and magic of it all. We can still marvel at the glorious randomness of this universe, especially when it works out in surprising and fortuitous ways for ourselves or those we care about. Just because there is a logical reason for something to have happened doesn't make it any less special.

I'm not sure if it's a result of being alive as long as I have or if the last three years have truly been extra hard, but I have watched so many people in my close circles suffering in new and terrible ways recently. Personally, I've dealt with two layoffs, extended unemployment, and a major spiritual, existential crisis. My husband developed mysterious medical symptoms, we think from the massive load of stress from his career coupled with his growing angst over my spiritual crisis. At one point, we were both self-employed, and neither one of us had any guaranteed income. In addition to all that, we had the regular struggles of raising tiny humans while maintaining our relationships, careers, health, and sanity during a global pandemic.

I have family members dealing with chronically, incurably sick kids, which has got to be the worst form of torture imaginable. One of my closest friends is dealing with terribly painful fertility issues, which has had a domino effect of damage on many other relationships in her life. Another close friend not only watched her mom nearly die from a massive stroke but also suffered an emotionally tortuous miscarriage two years later. I've watched multiple friends go through divorce; another friend had to put their baby under a surgeon's knife, and the worldwide pandemic took the lives of over one million Americans, including people I knew.

Many of these suffering people are faithful Christians. They pray, actively practice their faith, and ask for miracles—and what? God doesn't care? God cares but wants to use their suffering for some lesson or greater purpose? God cares but isn't moved enough to intervene, not yet anyway? God cares and is hurting in solidarity with them, but . . . it is what it is?

Miracles have always felt deeply unfair, if they're even real at all.

As my faith journey progressed, I had a harder and harder time praying. I didn't know what to say or what, if anything, to ask for. Should I ask for my family members to be healed? Or am I just supposed to pray for "God's will be done," whatever that mysterious will may entail? Was I trying to control God by praying for any specific outcome, or even worse, was that testing God? Jesus made it pretty clear during his scuffle in the desert with the Tempter that no one is meant to test God.[33]

So what do I say? Simply offer these people up and let God know I am upset on their behalf, that I love them and hate to see them suffering? That if *I* were an all-powerful, loving being, I couldn't possibly imagine idling by, knowing I had the power to make it better instantaneously?

Did I love my friends and family more than God?

I acknowledge the tension between a God who intervenes and a God who values free will above all else. How would those two differing modes of operation work together? Free will above all would suggest God allows humans to make their choices and expects them to deal with the consequences without intervention: a *laissez-faire* God who set the world in motion and then stood back to watch. But then miracles should never happen, and prayer requests would be useless. A God who intervenes, on the other hand, can show mercy but can also quickly become manipulative and controlling or play favorites. Maybe miracles were a weird loophole God used to get around interfering with our free will?

I've performed all kinds of mental gymnastics over the years to try to make it make sense:

➤ We're just all waiting out the clock for God to get fed up and begin the End Times, in which millions more people will supposedly die horrible deaths and some of us will end up in Eternal Bliss.

➤ God hates to see us suffering as much as we hate living it, but this is the broken, sinful world we live in. It'll get better in heaven.

➤ Humans are flawed and need tough love to learn from their mistakes. God can't make all our suffering go away, or they would be enabling us to continue in our sin.

➤ God feels our pain and is with us in it, but specific prayer requests are a gamble at best because we don't see the bigger picture from God's perspective.

➤ God longs for the world to be restored and for evil and suffering to be banished forever, and God is attempting to do work behind the scenes through the Holy Spirit, but God is counting on us to be their hands and feet to get that done. We had better hurry up, since all the millions of people still suffering around the world are stuck with the world as it is for now.

➤ Yes, God is Love itself, and God is all-powerful, but somehow God has set up this system in which they are limited and powerless to stop actual, atrocious suffering from happening because: free will.

Living in the chaos of the pandemic with more time at home to ponder these big thoughts about God, miracles, suffering, and love pushed me toward a breaking point. A world without God looked more realistic to me. I *wanted* to keep believing in God, I *wanted* to believe that prayer worked, I *wanted* to remain aligned with my husband, but I had thought things I couldn't unthink and had learned things I couldn't unlearn. I wasn't actively *trying* to undo everything I once believed; it felt like deconstruction was happening *to me*, almost against my will. I was reluctantly, yet resolutely, pushed forward. The cracks were breaking beyond repair. I was adrift on a floating piece of ice now, running out of time to make a break for the safe shoreline.

Free Will

THE SENSELESS MURDER OF TRAYVON Martin in 2012 broke my heart wide open. I could not fathom how an innocent boy walking through a neighborhood doing absolutely nothing wrong could be gunned down, and I was even more dismayed to watch his murderer go free! My shock led me to realize how woefully ignorant I was about the many ways that racist practices were built into the fabric of this country, from the birth of the police force to red lining and predatory loans to outright massacres and razing of successful Black communities like Tulsa, Oklahoma, and Seneca Village, New York. I have spent much of my thirties educating myself on racism in the U.S.A. The more I learned, the more horrified I became.[34]

I read about America's founding days and learned how enslaved Africans were a crucial part of America's economy since before America was an independent nation. I learned more about the hundreds of indigenous nations that were thriving on the continent first, how Europeans enslaved them as well, and of the endless broken treaties and purposeful deceptions committed against the tribes.[35] I read firsthand accounts of the horrors of slavery.[36] I learned about how awful things were with the botched Reconstruction era and the introduction of sharecropping, Jim Crow laws, and the modern version of slavery with the prison system.[37] I was shocked to discover that German Nazis had traveled to the Southern U.S. to study and learn how to get away with the Holocaust in broad daylight.[38] I learned about the continued theft, murder, and cover-ups perpetuated against indigenous tribes under the full awareness of the U.S. government.[39] My country committed a holocaust for *hundreds of years*, heinously torturing and murdering millions of people.[40]

When I first began to pay attention to social justice and suffering around the world during college, the primacy of free will explained evil to me. I thought that it was critical for God to allow humans to possess free will—that without it, our love and dedication meant nothing. Puppets on a string have no choice but to obey their master, and God wanted us to choose to love them of our own volition. So free will must be maintained at all costs, even when humans use that free will to make awful choices that cause harm to their fellow humans and the planet.

There is a philosophical debate out there on whether free will is real or not. Whether because of psychological priming, thoughts that seem to arrive in our brain without our conscious intent, or the inability to think a thought that is outside reality and our known experiences, a case can be made that free will does not truly exist.[41] fMRI studies show that the synapses in our brains start to fire before we can consciously articulate a thought[42]—was the thought planted in our head? Did we not truly choose to think or act ourselves if the process started before our awareness of it began?

Aside from the neurological debate, I certainly question the practicality of free will when it seems like the power to act on that will is hoarded by mere hundreds of powerful elites while *billions* of people end up subjected to their whims. Does the girl sold into sex trafficking have the choice to get out? Does she have any free will over the course of her life as she's fed drugs, moved around, kept disoriented and dependent on her pimp? I supposed you could say she has the will, but by no means the way. Those choices aren't available to her to make, no matter how much she wants them.

Do I—even as a middle-class, privileged white person in America—truly have the free will, practically speaking, to shop ethically? I care deeply about the people who make my clothes and have done the research, and it is nearly impossible to find clothing that I can guarantee is ethically produced. Twenty-two percent of raw cotton used to make clothing worldwide is currently coming from China, where the Uyghur people are being enslaved into the workforce.[43] It's a human rights nightmare, and it affects the textile industry worldwide. After the raw cotton is turned into fabric, the people stitching our clothes together tend to be treated unethically. The fashion industry is known for using cheap overseas labor in which fair practices and safe working conditions are not guaranteed. It is hard to even track that information and figure out where your favorite store gets their textiles from, let alone how they treat and compensate everyone involved in the process.

I do not have the knowledge or time to grow my own cotton, turn it into a usable product, and make my own clothes, so I'm essentially dependent on what's out there. And if the majority of what's out there is unethically made, where's my free will to choose otherwise? I do have the option to avoid buying new clothes and enabling these greedy companies, which is how I've handled that issue: I exclusively buy from secondhand shops. But the more I paid attention to politics and the capitalist empire, the more it looked to me like what we have is a small minority of people in power who have amassed wealth and influence and therefore get to play chess with everyone else's lives. Where's God? If absolute free will, practically and function- ally speaking, on a day-to-day basis in the actual lives of humans, doesn't really exist, then what does that mean about God? What is God's role there?

Since absolute free will seems restrained and we only truly have the free will to make choices within the narrow options available to us, well then, why can't God restrict those choices even further and rule out the options of choosing rape, murder, and abuse? I can imagine a world in which God could still leave the option up to us to choose to believe in them or not while restricting the potential for evil. With a supposedly all-powerful God creating the entire universe by speaking it into existence, imagining a better system than what we have is easy to do. Why would a lov- ing God create *this* world, *this* universe, in which sentient creatures are capable of such extreme violence?

Free will or not, I became unable to tolerate the idea of a god who would knowingly create a world capable of such evils. Events surrounding the murder of George Floyd became the schism point, creating a "before" and "after" in my spiritual life. I heard Floyd beg for his life with my own ears and watched his murder on the morning news. Incredibly horrific, incredibly pointless, incredibly wicked—and God knew it would be like this? That 157 years after slavery ended in this country, police would *still* be hunting down and murdering Black men in cold blood without following due process?

When news about George Floyd was current, I saw a lot of fellow white people waking up. Suddenly everybody was talking about racism and its continued, malevolent presence in our society in the U.S. I had been sadly watching the bodies stack up for years and had started to put up boundaries to prevent my heart from crashing altogether. So I had paid attention to Philando Castile's murder when it happened in 2016 in Minnesota, but I did not watch the video footage at the time.

After Floyd's murder, a friend shared the old video of Philando Castile's daughter and girlfriend sobbing in the backseat of the car in which he had just been gunned down by police. His daughter was about the age of my own young daughter, and her sweet, little voice begging her momma to stop yelling so the police wouldn't shoot her too, asking her mom why her city wasn't safer . . . it was too much.

God had been slowly fading into the mist, becoming more and more difficult to believe in over the recent months. At that moment, when I heard Philando Castile's daughter cry over the cold cruelty of this world, God fully disintegrated into nothingness. Poof. Gone.

Religious abuse and Christian hypocrisy never made me question God—I was able to explain away the awful things the church did by knowing that *human*s ran religious institutions. I could explain that the nefarious, pedophiliac sexual abusers were flawed humans and not actual place-holders for God in this world. Because church leaders include self-centered, power-hungry, insecure, greedy, flawed humans, I could understand why the church wasn't taking more drastic action to alleviate suffering in the world; wasn't fighting against entrenched racism, classism, and economic disparity; wasn't standing up for climate change reform to protect this beautiful world God supposedly made that is on the cusp of deadly metamorphosis. The human institution of religion was full of faults like every other human institution, but I was able to separate God from the institution.

I did, however, question how a God who claims to be the essence of Love itself could create a world in which people's bodies would be owned, raped, tortured, starved, worked to the bone, and killed by God's own people. The random suffering of cancer, incurable disease, mutilation, death by natural disasters, famine, and flood—God's pur-poseful world made all that too. I cannot fathom a God who knew the world they were creating would produce genocides, incest, starvation, sex trafficking, child abuse, American gun violence and dead elementary school chil-dren and didn't see fit to change the formula.

If that God exists, they are not worthy of my worship.

I know there is great beauty and love in the world, and that wonderful, kind, selfless acts happen every moment of every day. But the evil is very much present too. God sup-posedly knew how bad it was going to be in advance and was okay with that? No.

No.

Love couldn't do that. Love couldn't watch, *while supposedly being powerful enough to stop it,* while children got ripped from their parents in Native communities in America and Aboriginal communities in Australia to be "educated" in white systems that abused and killed them. Love couldn't stand by while six million Jewish people were grotesquely murdered by Nazi Germany. Love couldn't observe its beloved trans and gay children get bullied and murdered for being true to who they were made to be. Love couldn't tolerate watching all the nauseating, hideous things humans are capable of perpetuating on each other and the planet and patiently wait for justice. I could not continue to worship and follow any god who would knowingly create a world in which such evils exist.

I could no longer imagine a world in which there is an all-knowing, all-powerful, loving God lingering in the shadows. Watching. Occasionally intervening but hardly any of the time. Making us all jump through hoops during a brief lifespan on Earth before getting to the real show in the afterlife—why not just start our existence in heaven? Either that God is not as loving as we believe, or they are not as powerful, or not as wrapped up in the details of our lives—or they are a total liar.

It no longer made any sense.

Of course Love couldn't allow evil to go unchecked and watch their beloved children suffer horrifically every single day. Love wouldn't do that.

Love *didn't* do that.

Either God is not Love, or God is not real.

Any way you cut it, I was out.

I was terrified to admit that I no longer believed that God was real. My pulse quickened and my head buzzed when I was finally ready to articulate my thoughts. It truly felt like the most momentous decision I had ever made. My entire identity was wrapped around being a Christian. I wasn't sure who I would be anymore without God at the forefront of my life. I thought this would change *everything*.

I took the plunge. I allowed my belief in God to dissolve completely, and I was shocked to feel a deeper peace than I had ever known before. The lightning bolt never struck. After over thirty years of my intense devotion and discipleship, God didn't seem to care that I was leaving.

The ice beneath my feet shattered into a million pieces. I plunged into the dark waters of the cold world below. As I fell through the ice, through the looking glass, I knew that I couldn't go back. I felt terror and panic while sinking into the black void, but I noticed a curious sensation on the other side of the fear. For as frightened as I was of taking the plunge, of finally admitting to myself what I had suspected to be true for a while, I also felt a profound sense of calm alongside the fear.

It was a scary, new world under the ice, below the sunny surface, and yet I discovered peace. There was an honesty, a settled feeling, and a luminous glow from the depths that I was surprised to encounter. I found myself happy to float under the ice, surprised not to be frantically swimming for the surface. Maybe this new world had a place for me.

Maybe leaving the safe, smooth surface above and embracing what I had so greatly feared wasn't that bad.

I floated along in peace.

How could I feel this calm I felt after dropping the biggest bomb possible on my life? I had thought the sun would stop in the sky if I dared to deny God's existence, yet the Earth kept spinning. The cognitive dissonance I had been living with for my whole adult life suddenly dissipated. I had been going through life with a staticky radio constantly playing in the background that was suddenly switched off. Grief was on its way, but for the moment, the peace was palpable.

In giving up God, I gave up a formative part of my identity. I still had a lot of work to do to discover who I was without God at the helm. It was time to explore.

Looking Ahead

The greater the doubt, the greater the awakening.

C. C. Chang, *The Practice of Zen*

Floating

IT WAS TERRIFYING FOR ME to announce that I no longer thought there was such a thing as God. Forming the words with my mouth was physically difficult, and my heart raced wildly as I spit it out for the first time—to my ears alone! As calm as I felt about my personal decision, I was uncomfortable broadcasting it and felt nervous about the fallout. Telling my husband and closest friends was equally hard all over again each time. I would say it in hushed undertones and with cagey vocab, unable to be direct at first.

My husband was torn—he tried to be supportive and not overreact, but he was inwardly disturbed. We got married based upon our shared faith! He reacted with shock and denial, shoving the situation under the rug, and still hoped it wasn't permanent. None of my friends made a big scene when I told them. As I've said, all my closest friends are progressive, so they are comfortable with doubt and differing beliefs. I never made a large, public announcement, and I selectively chose who to inform. I'm sure some folks in my life would have reacted poorly, but I didn't feel the need to let them know what was happening. I held off telling my parents for a while, and they were understandably disturbed when they realized that I had left the faith.

We've had several uncomfortable conversations now, but they remain loving and supportive of me overall.

Since I hadn't believed in hell for some time, it wasn't eternal damnation I feared. I'd never had nightmares of going to hell as a child, although I often did worry about my relatives and friends who would be tortured forever. In my black-and-white understanding back then, I felt safe knowing I had prayed the prayer and was a "real Christian," according to my simple standards. The reason I felt intimidation now was that, in admitting I no longer believed in God, I had lost a monumental, massively influential part of my identity.

Who was I if I was no longer a Christian?

My identity had been completely subsumed in my faith. For my whole life, I hadn't taken credit or ownership over my own identity as I had been explicitly taught not to. The Bible says in Galatians 2:20, "I have been crucified with Christ. It is no longer I who live, but Christ who lives in me." I was supposed to be gone. I was supposed to be living for the kingdom of God, not for my own desires and dreams—unless, of course, I desired to be a missionary. I was supposed to dedicate my entire life to Christ. And I had swallowed that pill whole. That *had* been my goal for much of my young life.

After letting myself die with Christ, how was I to rise from the grave?

The voices I was so used to turning to weren't helping anymore. I am a huge fan of authors Sarah Bessey, Jen Hatmaker, Rachel Held Evans, Henri Nouwen, Richard Rohr, and Rob Bell. I used to turn to their books or their podcasts for comfort, guidance, reassurance, and to feel seen and known. I tried to read Rachel Held Evans's last book in 2021 but couldn't finish it. Jen Hatmaker's podcast left my Top 5 on Spotify. I tried reading the newest Shauna Niequist book, but her commentary on God's role in her tumultuous life felt shallow and false. These voices were no longer ringing true, and I found myself needing distance from them.

Rachel Held Evans, who suddenly died in 2019, often used to say, "On the days I believe this" about her faith.[44] I wished so badly that she was still around so I could follow along with her spiritual growth and investigate her honest thoughts on it all. Had she been going through a similar journey to mine? I will never know.

I felt lonely.

The first night that I went to bed and started to pray on autopilot stopped me dead in my tracks. An instant pin-prick of hot tears stung my eyes. It's hard enough to feel loneliness for other people—to feel loneliness for a Higher Being was intense. But I no longer believed anyone was listening to my prayers. The silence was deafening.

I thought about all the journals I had filled up over the years, full of prayers and ramblings meant for God's ears. And I remembered the sense of peace and clarity that I often got after writing about my problems. I felt comforted a little, thinking, if I am now correct to assume no one was ever listening, then I guess I was able to find a resolution to all those issues on my own. Meditating on the issue over the pages of my journals must have been inherently therapeutic, even without a divine therapist listening from the eaves.

The first major church holiday that came up after my personal schism was Christmas. The flagship Christian holiday. I was surprised to sail through that uneventfully. Christmas is so commercialized and easily more of a cultural event than a religious event, so I focused on the holiday aspects I liked about it: making Christmas cookies with the kids, decorating the house, driving around to see the lights, and attending the holiday events downtown; I left the religious significance of it all far in the background. My husband and I had not established overt religious rituals around Christmas yet, as our kids were just getting old enough to appreciate what was going on anyway. He was still in his denial phase concerning my beliefs, so we both maneuvered through the season on autopilot and didn't talk about it.

I did a little extra digging on the Christian appropriation of the many pagan aspects of the holiday. The symbolism of mistletoe and holly, the winter solstice, Saturnalia, and the yule log were interesting to learn about. While not wanting to become pagan or appropriate traditions that are not mine, I enjoyed learning about many indigenous customs and traditions regarding the holidays. Exploring these ancient human practices caused me to feel connected to the symbolism that humanity has long placed on these cyclical events in our lives.

When that first Easter rolled around, I found myself in a different place emotionally. As much as the Easter bunny and dying eggs have become standard (and there are Christian appropriations from pagan traditions for Easter too), Easter is hard to miss as a Christian religious event. I noticed I was getting irritable and cranky, and I spent most of the weekend in a funk. I commiserated with my friend who had also recently left the faith and was feeling similarly. As with all types of grief, my emotions over no longer believing in God will continue to come and go in fits and starts, and the best I can do is acknowledge the emotion, name it, and ride it out. I felt better by Monday, and time rolled on.

Shortly after Easter, my husband was finally jolted out of his denial when, after two-ish years of me talking this way, I didn't go up with him one week to receive communion at church. We hadn't been to church in person in so long due to the pandemic, and our church doesn't serve communion every week, so that was the first time I was confronted with what to do in that situation.

As an earnest believer, I never took communion lightly. Communion is a highly symbolic act rife with meaning, and I no longer believed the entire concept behind it. So I stayed in my pew, my husband went up alone, and then he sat back down and had a near panic attack. Mysterious symptoms that had manifested earlier during a period of increased stress that year roared back in full force. He was confronted with the reality that his wife was no longer a Christian, and he realized how upset he truly was. I felt terrible. Here I was, feeling deeper levels of peace and emotional health after resolving my cognitive dissonance, and he was in the unhealthiest place he'd ever been.

We met with our pastor and his wife to seek counseling. I respect my pastor deeply and had met up with him when my doubts were gaining strength to seek his opinion. He was not offended or threatened by my questions and even related to me quite a bit. So I trusted his opinion and was happy to meet with them to work things out in my marriage. As my husband shared our situation and his concerns, it became clear that much of his stress was coming from work. My spiritual changes certainly affected him, yet another straw to add to the camel's back, but were not the only source of his suffering. We were encouraged to keep openly communicating and to work together to redefine things in our marriage.

We still have many talks ahead of us as we figure out a new way of being a couple and how to raise our kids. We both went to therapy over all this and will continue seeking out healthy pathways forward, such as reading new books and seeking out new voices while we figure out how to reorient our relationship. After having an easy, smooth marriage from the beginning, this is the most difficult thing we've dealt with. It isn't going to be nicely resolved in a predictable time frame. We're in brand-new territory.

For the time being, I am still attending church with my family, for several reasons. I love and care for my husband, and going to church as a family is meaningful for him. I want to be supportive, even if that's not where I would choose to spend my time on Sunday morning. I've attended other events and activities with him that I wouldn't have chosen to attend on my own; I think that's part of marriage.

I also deeply respect my local church. While initially meeting with my pastor to discuss my questions, he never made me feel judged or unwelcome, and he was open about many of his deep-seated doubts. My church is open and affirming to all sexual and gender identities; is egalitarian with women serving as pastors, preachers, and elders on the board; has entire sermon series on doubt and other hot topics within both the church and society like sex, money, and racism; and is leading and teaching us to be the kind of human I still want to be.

I think it's healthy for my continued development as a human being to go somewhere once a week and listen to a talk that may challenge me to think differently, to look inward, and to be motivated or convicted to change something about my behavior or lifestyle for the better. Church fills that role for me and remains a viable option for now. I still want the inherent accountability that comes from being a part of a community. I still want to gather regularly with a group of people because sometimes something magical happens when a bunch of people get together. Most of my church's values still mirror my own: I'm simply approaching them from a different motivation at this point.

Just recently, during my current stage of complete disbelief, I attended church and looked around at all the familiar faces. People were smiling, greeting each other, and hugging, and as they started singing a beautiful song with two women up front harmonizing gloriously, I felt my heart swell with a deep, meaningful love for all humanity. I've had similar feelings at other large events, and that sensation of wide-open love and acceptance and being part of the "oneness" that is humanity is always a welcome feeling. I didn't believe the Holy Spirit was moving in my heart (as I would have in the past), but I enjoyed the community and transcendent moment nonetheless.

As for my kids, I want them to have the option of such a strong foundation as I was blessed with in my youth. We don't focus on sin, hell, or judgment, but rather on the idea that they are inherently loved by God. Like I said earlier, being a Christian made me who I am in a good way, a way that I would be happy to pass along to my kids, not to mention that there's a chance I'm wrong and God is real. This may sound demeaning, but I'm okay with perpetuating what may be a misunderstood half-truth to my kids while they are young. We do Santa and the Easter bunny at my house—a loving God who cares about them deeply can be another beautiful part of their childhood. As they mature, my husband and I will have to decide when I should be more fully honest with them in sharing my beliefs. In a similar way, we only teach them the bare basics of reproduction at this stage of their lives, and we answer many of their million questions in incomplete truths. I don't need to get deep into the inner workings of my spiritual state right now; it wouldn't be developmentally appropriate for them.

At the same time, we've been open with my children about the many other religions out there. We read baby board books on Islam and Hanukkah and Diwali. We've read beautiful books on Zen Buddhism, Native American beliefs, and indigenous Hawaiian spirituality. One of my daughter's friends from school mentioned that she and her family don't go to church, which I used as an opportunity to tell my daughter that other people don't believe all the same things we believe. Whenever we encounter a person from a show, book, or real life who has a different background, I draw attention to their culture or religion and use it as a teaching opportunity. One of our family mottos is "You can always change your mind!" We talk about the fact that it's okay to ask questions and okay to think differently. I will keep exposing them to other ideas and beliefs and ways of being human, and eventually, I will encourage them to decide for themselves what to believe.

AS I FULLY STEPPED AWAY from my faith and into a brand-new, unknown space, I felt completely alone while trying to piece together a new way to exist in the world. My friends with whom I had discussed my spiritual status were understanding and supportive, but they were not asking the same questions I now had. On the other hand, I have had a dear friend for over a decade who's been an atheist that entire time whom I could now turn to for discussions on life and meaning from this naturalistic perspective, but he couldn't relate to my grief. My other friend who walked away from his faith at nearly the same time I did, but for much different, more personal reasons, could relate to a degree but occupied a different emotional space than myself. We were grieving in different ways, although talking with him and his wife—who still identifies as a Christian, as does my husband—has been helpful for my marriage as we all navigate these new waters. I am discovering my new path through the best way I know how: voraciously hunting down knowledge and information. After reading C.S. Lewis, Philip Yancey, Donald Miller, Shane Claiborne, and all the other many wonderful books about Jesus and the Bible that I've consumed over the years, I am now reading a whole new set of books and listening to new voices in my podcasts and slowly piecing together a new framework for living in this world.

While I would like to flesh that out a little here to offer a different way for those looking, I am hesitant to act as if I've now discovered the "real truth" or correct answers about anything. I am wary of falling into a new black-and-white universe that is governed by science and facts versus faith. Thankfully, science itself is humble by nature, always striving for objectivity and open to change when new information becomes available.

By leaning into the gray zones, into the mysterious, into the wonderful complexities of the universe, I struggle to wrap a label around it all. I don't want to do that, nor do I think it's a good approach. I hope as I've led you down this winding road with nerdy asides about paleoanthropology and neurophysiology that I've woven all the random stories and education from my last fifteen years of spiritual investigation together into a tapestry of faith, doubt, wonder, and loss. But I've deliberately left the big bow off as I can't wrap this all up with a nice, tidy ending. My story is still being written, as is yours. I will keep reading, keep questioning, keep learning and growing, and I am so curious to see where I'll be and what I'll believe in another fifteen years.

NATURE HAS ALWAYS HELD A special allure for me. I grew up in a busy suburb of Chicago, but several times a year my family would go camping in our ugly old Coleman pop-up. We're talking an orange and brown plaid interior in a bold stand of solidarity with the '70s during the middle of the '90s. I loved everything about our camping trips. I loved setting up the camper with my dad, loved hiking to the bathroom, loved the smell of my mom's Noxzema as we washed up together before bed, and loved how goofy and carefree my family became with no work schedules or obligations to fill the day.

Mostly, I loved being outside twenty-four hours a day since the only "inside" was our canvas-walled camper through which sounds of savage animals (and the occasionally savage neighboring camper) easily passed. From an early age I have felt a spiritual connection to the great outdoors. I sensed a sacred space in the forests of the Appalachian Mountains, on the sand dunes of Michigan, at South Carolina's Atlantic shores, in the rocky canyons of Utah, and on top of the Rocky Mountains of Colorado. Hiking around these beautiful landscapes caused me to feel both small and intricately connected to my surroundings, a tiny part of a greater whole. My response used to be to praise God for the wonder and beauty of nature. My perspective on being one part of this greater whole has now changed, but the feeling remains.

After breaking up with God, I'm experiencing a passionate rebound with the Great Outdoors. Nature remains a deep love of mine, even more after learning what I have recently about evolution and our prehuman ancestors. I still feel a sense of sacredness as I've been exploring my adopted home of the Pacific Northwest. Heck, I have "spiritual moments" when outside in my own backyard, when the breeze makes the leaves dance on the big maple tree and the sun kisses my skin just right. I love being outside, and I have learned a lot about life from nature over the years.

DURING MY SEMESTER ABROAD IN Australia, I was lucky enough to take a spring break trip to Fiji. "*Bula!*" I stepped off the plane to the sounds of a steel drum and the caress of a tropical breeze. Greeters waited in the airport lobby with shell necklaces and sunny smiles to welcome newcomers to this tropical paradise. I was in Fiji! The island of Viti Levu will forever conjure up images of paradise in my mind's eye.

I spent nine days exploring the island while on board the Fee Jee Experience tour bus. The tour was fantastic: a leisurely loop around the island, complete with sandy picnics, jungle hikes, river rafting, and village visits. The trip flew by too quickly, and I was sad to have it come to an end. The penultimate night of the Fee Jee Experience took our group into the heart of the island to visit the mud pits in an enterprising farmer's sugarcane fields. The bus plowed down the farmer's driveway and parked us sunburnt and sweating tourists right in his front yard.

Our tour guide, Didi, was one of those women whose age is impossible to guess. She must have been over fifty years old, but her hyperactivity, youthful giggle, buttery skin, and spry figure made it hard to say. She got the group pumped up for these mud pits, singing their praises as the Fijian fountain of youth. She herself took a dip in the silky soil once a week as part of the tour, perhaps contributing to her age-defying complexion.

As we picked our way through the sugarcane, the farmer's children sneaking peeks and giggling at all of us tomato-skinned tourists, I had my doubts. This smacked of gimmick, trying to help a local out by bringing in some foreign currency. We came to the first mud pit, and it was just that—a sloppily circular hole in the earth filled with muddy water. The first brave tourists got in and immediately sunk to their waists in the murky bottom. Didi instructed everyone to join them and to slather ourselves with the mud from the bottom of the pool. We all quickly followed, flinging mud at one another, passing along mud-massages and facials. We became the Fijian version of the Swamp Thing while connecting with our inner three-year-old selves!

After we were thoroughly coated in mud, Didi had us all climb out of that pool and head across the field to another, clearer pool with mist lightly rising from its surface. Following our exotic mud bath, we got to cleanse ourselves in a natural hot spring. Fortunately, the sun had recently set, and the night was cooling off, so the steaming water felt delicious. Gently splashing and lounging in the purifying waters, I felt reborn. And gimmick or not, my skin felt as smooth as a baby's cheek after that Fijian mud was rinsed off.

However, the most amazing part of this night was yet to come. After toweling off and reluctantly climbing back into the tour bus, we headed off to our last hostel of the tour. I was in such a state of bliss and contentedness that I could hardly feel sad that the trip was almost over. I needn't have worried. Less than half the distance back to the main road, the tour bus broke down. Now, this was the second time that this had happened—the first instance came about from an intriguing case of sabotage after the bus driver, during a moment of clarity while partying hard with the group the night before, had destroyed the engine in a selfless act of group preservation. That bus driver was no longer with us, and his replacement insisted that this bus had died from natural causes.

No one panicked or worried as we filed out of the bus to wait at the side of the road. "Road" may not be the right word; it was more like two tire-wide lanes of dirt parting the grass for the sole purpose of bringing tour buses to the mud pits and the farmer to market. We all climbed up the small embankment and made ourselves comfortable, lying among stalks of sugarcane. The stars were sparkling in a velvety black sky in an exhibit that would have rivaled any jewelry store display case. As I gazed overhead and enjoyed the scent of warm earth in my nose and the caressing breeze on my baby-soft skin, I heard a gentle sound in the distance.

Sitting up, I saw a fire-lit hut in the field across the lane. Through the open doorway I could see at least three generations of a family sitting around one of the younger sons, who held a drum in his lap. They were singing. On a Saturday evening, Grandmother, Mother and Father, teenagers and baby were all gathered, happily singing a sweet, tropical melody.

My heart about melted right then.

This family spending their free evening together, hanging out and singing, was the most vivid picture of community I had ever seen. I was not so naive to think that this family coexisted in perfect peace all the time, but in that moment, they were tranquility defined. They were the perfect image of heaven to me.

When I sit still and spend time with those I love, paying attention to the moment, singing songs on a warm summer evening or talking in front of the fireplace while snow buries the front yard, I am filled with peace and joy. I think living close to the natural world and apart from technology, as I saw firsthand in Fiji, has a way of bringing people together. Part of the fun of my childhood camping trips was being off the grid, away from TVs and phones and computers. With all the distractions at bay, we were forced into the present moment. Living in the present is a gift that nature continues to teach me as I learn to manage the random trials and tribulations of life.

If I am stressed at work, flustered by a patient who is not progressing as I had hoped, and I remember to breathe and connect to the present moment, I feel an instant wave of relief. My perspective is expanded, and I am reminded of the big picture of things. Then my brain is better able to think critically and creatively since it is not bogged down with thoughts of inadequacy and feelings of frustration.

If I am caught in traffic and rushing to get home so I can unwind and relax, I naturally find myself changing lanes and unsuccessfully trying to beat the crowd (I did learn to drive in Chicago). Occasionally on those days, a sound, a smell, or a sunbeam grounds my thoughts into *now*. I feel the tension in my shoulders dissipate as I slow down and look at all the others on the road as fellow humans who are also eager to get home to their families. And I relax and listen to a podcast or find a good song on the radio or turn it off and sometimes even enjoy the extra time to myself to think.

If I am caught in an anxious mindset about my spiritual upheaval and the ripples it's causing in my family, and I stop and watch my kids play or get outside and get into my body, I experience a calm shift in perspective. This way I'm able to shelve my divine worries and eternal concerns and enjoy the present moment with intention.

Throughout my life, nature has patiently and gradually taught me mindfulness. Time slowed down when I eagerly watched the skies for lightning during a Midwestern thunderstorm. My thoughts quieted while I sat at the beach and watched the sunset over the water during my summers as a lifeguard. I appreciated the present moment with my whole body when I savored the feeling of sun on my skin and wind in my hair. Watching the light dance over the unbelievably teal surface of a glacial lake in Montana made me speechless with awe. My easily distracted brain focused when I followed the joyful and erratic path of a butterfly through my backyard.

Nature is a fantastic instructor and inspires me to slow down, to breathe deeply, and to savor all the beauty and wonder this life contains.

Meaning

AFTER I TOOK THE PLUNGE into atheism and started looking
for a new life philosophy, I discovered *The Big Picture: On the
Origins of Life, Meaning, and the Universe Itself* by Sean
Carroll. Carroll is a theoretical physicist at the California
Institute of Technology. His book was pivotal in helping me
find a new framework through which to view the world after
God left the picture. The book illustrated what science has
taught about the "how" of all this. Carroll used science to
explain, with a high amount of certainty, how the universe
started, spread, and ultimately created the Earth and humanity as we know it today. His book was overwhelmingly thorough in its attempt to explain . . . everything. It gave me a
greater appreciation for all science has done as well as a better
framework to understand the differences between fundamental, elemental truths and what he called "emergent truths."

I latched onto this idea of emergent truths to reframe
both why I had believed in God for so long and why I had
now stopped. I was able to see through a new lens and understand where I had come from and envision where I wanted to
go next. Emergent truth works this way: think of the surface
you are sitting on. If you are sitting on a chair, can you say
that it is the object's fundamental truth to be a chair specifically? Isn't it wood that you are sitting on? Or rather, the

wood is made of fibrous tissues of cellulose. Cellulose is in turn made of molecules, which are composed of atoms, which are made up of electrons and protons and neutrons—which are made from quarks. Electrons and quarks seem to be the smallest building block of physical matter that we've discovered. So, the chair you are sitting on is, fundamentally, a collection of quarks and electrons. *You* are a collection of quarks and electrons. Plants, animals, people, and bowling balls are all essentially a collection of quarks and electrons.

The fundamental truth is that your chair is a collection of quarks and electrons assembled into atoms, then molecules, then cells, governed by the laws of thermodynamics, particle physics, quantum physics, the fundamental laws of mechanics, and the like. Strong and weak forces hold the molecules together, giving you a stable surface to sit on, but they are ultimately tiny particles.

The emergent truth is that you are sitting on a chair. "Chair" is a concept we've invented to communicate more clearly and make sense of this world. A chair is not an elemental part of the universe. A chair can look a thousand different ways. Objects that we think of as chairs can also be used as stools or tables. Other objects that typically have a different job to do can also serve as chairs, like your kitchen counter or the trunk of your car. "Chair" is a loose concept: an emergent truth with a made-up definition that we modify at will.

At a fundamental level, we are simply quarks and electrons, and yet we are so much more than quarks and electrons. Atoms don't have wants or emotions. Atoms can't think about the future and fall in love. We are something more than our component parts, as is the rest of the greater universe. Through some incomprehensible magic, a mass of rapidly dividing cells hits a point where they collectively become something greater, something with consciousness, something capable of love and creativity. I was able to see that as groups of humans grew and multiplied, they too became something greater than their component parts, something with governments, something capable of the arts, capable of developing elaborate cultures.

As early humans became more advanced, we needed to create a system to help share our ideas, and language was born. As our understanding of the world and our societies became more and more complex, we needed larger concepts to help explain everything. We needed systems of talking about things that made it easier to communicate, so we developed ideas of mathematics, emotions, governments, etc. Human society has developed emergent truths that govern our reality and our behavior. They may not be fundamentally real, but they are *real*, practically speaking.

An example Carroll gave in his book concerned the rules of playing basketball. The rules around basketball are not a fundamental truth of the universe. They are man-made, changeable, and arbitrary. However, to play a successful game of basketball, all the players must agree to the rules, or there would be chaos. The rules are *real* in that sense. We created rules to make sense of the world, or in this case, to make sense of a group of people running up and down a court with a ball and two baskets.

This same principle goes for traffic laws, currency, governments, ethics, social norms, and (I dare say) religion. None of those ideas are foundational building blocks of the universe, and yet we need them for society to function. We created those rules and systems to bring order to our world. I do not believe that a Higher Being who created the universe for a purpose and knows everyone on an individual level is a fundamental piece of the fabric of the universe. In all my research, I have not seen any evidence of a missing particle, force, or energy where God is required to fill the gap and explain any part of the universe and how things work. In fact, I've learned from actual scientists that there is no "god gap." The idea of Something Greater than all this that provides purpose and brings order to our lives is an emergent truth. Humanity has advanced so much in our mental and emotional capacity to ask questions and wonder about ourselves and the world, and we have created an emergent truth called God to explain how things are. And I know, from personal experience, that God has the potential to serve a wonderful purpose. My former belief in a Higher Being imbued me with a sense of humility, of worth and personal value, of wonder, of love and hope. My faith provided a moral and ethical compass through which to navigate the world.

I saw that religion functions to categorize and further organize thoughts about this emergent concept of a Higher Being. Diverse societies around the world developed ideas of a spiritual realm and each came up with unique ways of ritualizing and codifying their beliefs into various religious practices. Religions are as varied and diverse as humanity itself. Estimates put the number of current religious practices at over four thousand.[45] Going back in time, there are countless religious practices and beliefs that have come and gone through the ages. Because I live in the twenty-first century, it seems obvious to me that the ancient Greeks, for example, made up Zeus and Hades and all the others. After all, most people today aren't going to temples to worship Athena or pay homage to Apollo. Yet just like the people of today, the people in that day struggled to make sense of the way things are and came up with a complex, multilayered, fascinating set of gods and other supernatural beings that still inspire us (and Hollywood) today.

The emergent truths embodied in religion started simply and gained complexity throughout the ages. The Norse people of old created Thor in part to explain weather events. The ancient Egyptians believed the sun god Ra drove his chariot across the sky to create each day. Mormonism, created by Joseph Smith to correct what he saw as false teaching within Christianity, has a complex backstory and set of rules that direct the lives of over sixteen million people worldwide. Science fiction author L. Ron Hubbard created Scientology, which is comprised of complex hierarchies and systems. It's easy to look at belief systems other than our own and see them for the man-made systems they are. But if we turn our gaze inward, we can realize that even our own spiritual beliefs are emergent truths humans use to try to understand the world and give meaning to our lives.

Maybe there is a fundamental truth to a Higher Being existing, but no one religion has fully understood it yet.

Maybe some get certain pieces or aspects correct while missing out on other components. I am willing to entertain that idea because there are still mysteries out there, but I'm not holding my breath on the reality of a god-being.

Maybe humans have always created gods and systems of belief as emergent truths—and doubled down on those beliefs due to confirmation bias—because we *want* structure in an otherwise uncaring, random world. Maybe as soon as our early ancestors were capable of deep thoughts and difficult questions, they started creating answers to those questions, even if fundamental answers never existed. Maybe we came up with gods the same way we came up with governments and commerce—a way to give direction to our lives.

Maybe, on the other hand, the universe is simply a self-evident reality: we are here because we are here with no further explanation, a product of evolution without a Creator or purpose behind it all—and just because we *want* there to be more doesn't mean there *is* anything more than this. Maybe this present moment and this material world are all we are guaranteed to know to be absolute truth. Maybe we really do live in an uncaring, random universe with no one in charge and no purpose or plan behind it all.

Maybe.

At first, the thought that humans had created the concept of God, and subsequent religious practices, made me feel aimless. A godless world seemed empty and pointless to me. If no one is watching our lives or cares about the outcome, then what's the point?

But are our lives really set up only to be performative? Do we only behave for an audience? Can't we live for the sake of living, for our own selves, for our satisfaction and enjoyment? Can't we be grateful for the mysterious gift of life we've been given and strive to make the most of it without the promise of an afterlife?

Morality is not dependent upon the existence of God. Morality still exists in a godless world because we have created systems of morality to govern our lives and provide structure for society. I can reject the emergent truth of the Christian religion while adhering to other emergent truths, such as humanism or basic morality, that bring goodness to my life.

I also wasn't initially sure how to define meaning or right living without God providing my moral framework. However, learning about emergent truth allowed me to see that the lack of a Higher Being doesn't signify that there is no purpose to our lives. Our lives matter because we are here, alive! Living, breathing, thinking, loving beings who can affect the world and people around us for better or for worse.

We create meaning.

We give our lives meaning through our values and actions, in our relationships, and with our impact on the world.

Sometimes I think about people who lived uneventful lives in the year 857 CE or 1682 BCE (I'm a weird kid). Not the kings and heroes whose names we remember, but the normal folks—friends, mothers, healers, farmers, builders. They lived and died, and no single person alive has any clue about them today. But they *mattered* at their time. They loved and were loved, they helped their neighbors and contributed in whatever small way to society. They mattered in the particular—in their specific setting—even though in the great, big picture they might not have had much impact. Although you never know—that one kind person who helped someone else in their moment of struggle may have created the boost that person needed to go on and do something world-changing. The butterfly effect is real, y'all.

I was taken by a story Carroll told concerning the death of Carl Sagan—a famous astronomer, astrophysicist, cosmologist, and atheist. He shared a large quote from Sagan's widow, Ann Druyan. She spoke beautifully about the finality of Carl's death. She explained that she did not believe that she would ever get to see or communicate with Carl again. Being aware of that made their lives all the sweeter. The lack of purposeful design to the universe didn't make everything meaningless but rather infused their lives with profound significance. They viewed every moment as a miraculous gift and cherished their precious time together. She said, "I don't think I'll ever see Carl again. But I saw him. We saw each other. We found each other in the cosmos, and that was wonderful."[46] What a beautiful perspective.

Rob Bell wrote a book titled *Everything Is Spiritual: Who We Are and What We're Doing Here,* which I read and enjoyed. He argues that there is this false divide between the real world and the spiritual world and gives several stories of beautiful, transcendent moments in his life that happened during secular activities, claiming that those moments are as spiritual as any church experience. He discusses quantum mechanics and the expansion of the universe, how we're all particles and atoms—the interconnectedness of all things—and he says, "Everything is Spiritual. You've always belonged, the whole thing is an endless invitation."[47] To me, it feels like he's explaining poetic naturalism—which I'll get into more in an upcoming chapter—from the opposite side of the coin.

In saying everything is spiritual, Bell argues that this physical world that we live in, this world ordered and governed by scientific laws, still contains mystery, and beauty, and glorious coincidences, and a phone call just when we need to hear someone's voice, and all sorts of heart-wrenching happiness when we're least expecting it. That every moment of every ordinary day can be filled with profound meaning. The way he uses the word *spiritual* to me is really describing *meaning*. Every ordinary moment can be meaningful, even outside of religious or overtly spiritual experiences.

We create our own meaning within and outside of religion all the time. When something bad happens, we can decide that we are being challenged and use that to motivate us, to feel our character tested, and to rise above. I can take my horrible performance at golf as a personal challenge to my character—testing how committed I am to growth and improvement. Or I can decide it's only a stupid game that I happen to suck at and who cares about golf anyway? No greater meaning there, just a hobby I'll never take up.

We can look at a struggle and decide that we are being punished for some fault. For the longest time, for example, birth defects were viewed as a punishment for the parents or the child from a past life, assigning cruel meaning to random genetic mutations, claiming they were judgment on that person's character. Or we could realize that defects happen randomly without any purpose or moral reflection upon the afflicted.

Self-defined meaning—our emergent truth—isn't necessarily false or fraudulent. The significance we attribute to whatever happens to us is not any less true than the rules of basketball are true while playing a game. I can acknowledge that the universe is pointless and random and still decide that my life and my experiences are meaningful. There doesn't need to be an actual, intelligent, loving, or even vengeful Higher Being to make sense of the world. Things happen to us and around us due to a million factors such as other people's choices, natural phenomena, biology, and pharmacology, but we get to choose how to deal with the randomly good and randomly bad things that come our way.

In one sense, this is a powerless view of the world—our lives entirely at the whim of an uncaring, unpredictable universe that isn't aware of or invested either way regarding our well-being. No one to pray to and petition for help. No one to step in with a miracle to save the day. No statements of faith to make or merit badges to earn to get a seat in Paradise. Yet I find this idea of a random universe much more palatable when it comes to evil and suffering. It felt awful to think there was a God above who was watching and allowing such horrible things to happen without interfering most of the time. The belief that no one is watching and that life is a random crapshoot of good and bad events allows suffering to make more sense to me. No longer viewing trials and tribulations as punishment or a divine challenge to rise above, I am free to take life as it comes.

In the completely opposite sense, I also find it empowering to view the world as totally random. Without the stringent laws of religion controlling our behavior and choices, we have the freedom to act in any way we desire. Hopefully most of us choose to act in law-abiding ways that take care and consideration of others into account, but now we have the freedom to make choices our religion may not have allowed. We can love whomever we are drawn to love. We can present ourselves to the world in whatever way feels natural and truest to us, regardless of how society may have defined and categorized us. We can form relationships or leave relationships based on what serves us best and how we feel most alive. We can center ourselves and our own lives as opposed to living for some Divine Being or an arbitrary set of values.

It is difficult for me to think of living completely for myself. I was trained all my life not to be selfish, to follow God at all costs—which usually meant dying to some aspect of myself—and to suffer for the kingdom of God. I struggle now to create a healthy new approach to centering myself in my own story without feeling slimy. Because there is nuance there.

There is an unhealthy side to a "me first" approach to life, even though putting myself first at times allows me to live my best life and be both a better spouse and a better parent. I see beauty in moments of selflessness, but total selflessness with a complete lack of personal boundaries leads to bitterness and resentment. Yet most acts of heroism are selfless in nature, with heroes risking their lives to save complete strangers. Social progress through civil rights and suffrage was achieved by folks who put the big picture and greater good of society ahead of their own personal safety and well-being. I am still working out how to balance being true to myself and living for myself with looking out for others, for my family and friends.

I also don't fully know how to handle social norms as many of the ones I'm accustomed to were founded on religious beliefs. Should they all burn to the ground, or is there something good in standardizing behavior? At least some behaviors? Certainly the non-binary community suffers greatly from being coerced to follow the current gender norms that society demands. At the same time, I would not advocate for normalizing public masturbation, no matter how much that may support individuals centering themselves and their desires at all given moments; some social norms save us all from a lot of discomfort and insult. I'm still working out the best way to be human, as we all are every day.

Overall, I was drawn to the concept of emergent truth because it acknowledges that humanity has created social norms, customs, and cultures that define meaning for our species. Emergent truth requires no God above to dictate or restrict our behavior; instead, our societies continually create and recreate what it means to be human. We as individuals can choose to live this one precious life of ours however we see fit.

Within our realm of control, we can choose to react to the randomness of life from a place of health, and wholeness, and peace—or not. Certain folks have more resources, power, and influence and can handle struggles from a place of privilege compared to others. Some folks are fighting serious physiological and biochemical challenges that make a positive outlook and ambitious behavior extremely difficult. Whole groups of people are fighting against centuries of concerted political and social efforts to keep them down. We don't share equal amounts of control over our lives.

However, I *can* work on controlling my own posture toward blessings and curses. I can choose to allow getting laid off twice in one year during a global pandemic to get me down and depressed, unmotivated to move forward. And, after processing the grief, I can strive to pivot and reimagine my career path and start looking outside of the box. It is appropriate to be sad, mad, or discouraged when bad things happen—and equally important to move through those emotions and to keep moving forward when ready.

Likewise, I can choose to allow a medical diagnosis to cause me to give up and quit trying, or I can work to stay optimistic, surround myself with supportive friends and family, stick to the best medical plan possible, and hope for the best. I can choose to invite others into my struggles to help ease my burdens. I can keep seeking out resources and information to find the best path forward, or I can choose to give in to misery and wallow in my bad fortune—which is a viable option, though one not lifted up by societal standards. We do have agency over our choices and actions. We can't simply choose for the problem to stop, can't make the issue evaporate, but within the realm of possibility, we have some control.

There is still room for hope in a world without God.

I do my best not to take what life throws at me personally. When things work out well, I'm grateful. When things go badly, I grieve and keep at it or try something new.

I was able to put this into practice when we took our kids on a trip to Glacier National Park for their birthdays. I pumped the trip up for months leading up to it. We rented a sweet AirBnB on the shore of Lake McDonald inside the park, an option I didn't know existed until this trip. I hadn't been there in eleven years and was *so excited* to share my favorite place on this planet with my kids. About a week before the trip, I was on the GNP website getting excited and planning which hikes to attempt when I saw a banner that I hadn't noticed before.

"Construction!"

The Going-To-The-Sun road—the only road through the park—closed for construction the week prior to our arrival. It hadn't been announced with much notice, or I would have reconsidered booking the trip. We wouldn't be able to access over 90% of the park.

We decided to go anyway and explore the sliver of the western edge that was available to us.

While approaching nightfall during the drive out there, our car's check engine light started flashing when we were fifteen miles outside the city of Kalispell, still an hour away from our destination. I pulled over. While my husband popped the hood and looked around (at nothing since it's all computerized these days), a truck drove up and rolled its window down. As we explained our situation, the driver informed us that if the check engine light is *flashing*, it is safe to drive to get to a shop ASAP. I frantically Googled and called around to find a shop that would still be open and could help us. We cruised into the parking lot of a dealership that was able to examine our car and loan us a rental right before they closed for the night so that we could still go on our vacation. We transferred all our gear, ripped the car seats out, secured them in the rental, and kept going on our way.

Despite so many initial barriers popping up, we were still able to enjoy a gorgeous, relaxing, special vacation. We explored parts of the park I would have never otherwise visited. We enjoyed leisurely mornings and spent hours throwing rocks into Lake McDonald instead of rushing around the park to see specific sights. We took jaunts over to the nearby towns of Whitefish and Polebridge to explore what was there. The slow pace we were forced into ended up being so relaxing and put us all in such good moods that we were hardly bothered when we learned that our car needed a whole new engine. Thankfully, it was covered by our warranty, and we were able to keep the rental until our car was ready. My husband did have to drive back to Kalispell on the now snowy mountain passes (a ten-hour round trip that ate up his entire Saturday) to pick our car up when it was finished. Not ideal. But instead of letting the roadblocks stop us from having a good time, we were able to not take it personally or as a sign from above that the trip was cursed. We reimagined what the trip could look like and had a terrific time.

In my new godless world, I found freedom. The concepts I learned from Carroll's book were pivotal for me to reframe my worldview and find hope again. They helped me to find a new way to conceptualize meaning, value, and morality. I felt a stronger sense of agency as I realized that I could create my own definition for what constitutes a good life. I discovered that I didn't need God to have a fulfilling, purposeful life. I now know that my own unique definition of meaning is up to me to create and recreate throughout my life. What a gift.

I HAD ANOTHER TRANSCENDENT MOMENT with nature during my visit to Fiji. The tour had taken me around to the north side of the island where the beach-front hostel offered SCUBA dives. I eagerly signed up. With no previous diving experience, I was more frightened than reassured by the shallow water safety session. Getting jostled by the waves in four feet of cloudy water while practicing how to get the regulator back in my mouth in case of an emergency was far from comforting, not to mention that our Fijian instructors with their laid-back island attitude did not appeal to my American sense of structure, order, and liability coverage.

After what felt like a mere twenty minutes of practice and signing my life away in a simple release form, I jumped on board the boat to head toward the "Dream Maker" dive sight.

With a heavy oxygen tank strapped to my bare back and my heart racing, I tipped backward off the boat and into the warm Pacific. Even in the depths, the water was warm enough that we didn't need wet suits. We got to dive wearing our bikinis and feel the currents flowing past our skin. I began my first descent, and after two minutes of remaining under the surface without coming up for air, I began to panic. The human body is not meant to breathe underwater! Every cell in my body knew this and rebelled against my efforts to fool nature. I sputtered my way to the surface and splashed around for a while, trying to regain my cool.

One of our leather-skinned, Buddha-bellied Fijian instructors swam over to me with a smile in his eyes, calmly grabbed my hand, made sure my regulator was cleared and in place, and pulled me under. We held hands for the first ten feet down into the ocean depths, and I have never felt more secure or safe. Gone were the feelings of panic, the fears of getting trapped far below the surface with no hope of returning to the open air. I was SCUBA diving!

A whole new world opened up to me. I felt like an intruder on another planet or in a magical new dimension. I spied on a huge school of fish that turned and encircled me in a mesmerizing dance to the music of the universe. My astonished eyes roamed over the most intricate, delicate sculptures of coral that burst out in huge, fanned formations from large rocks and underwater canyons. I almost gasped and lost my lifeline when one of the Fijians pointed out some coral that changed color when "tickled" by agitating the water around it.

For deep sea companions, there were fish colored with a rainbow paintbrush, sea cucumbers, and electric blue starfish. I stood on the ocean floor forty-five feet below the surface and gawked like a tourist. My life was changed. Could I pull a reverse Little Mermaid and trade my legs in for fins? I never wanted to leave this magical place. There was too much to see! Off in the distance, past the huge coral formations, the ocean floor stretched out, dark and beckoning.

When our forty-five minutes were up, my friend and I were the last to surface and nearly had to be dragged up in a 180° reversal of my handheld descent. We made eye contact through the glass of our goggles while we waited to decompress and did not need to speak to share in the wonders we had witnessed. We rejoined the terrestrial realm with reluctance.

Billions of people will go their entire lives without ever experiencing the ocean depths the way I did. That complete oblivion struck me as profound. Here was this entire world that I had never known existed. All this wonder, beauty, and music had been there every day, and I was totally unaware. Our planet is a beautiful, diverse place, and it is huge.

The natural world seems so magical and divine to me because there is so much of it. There is always something new to discover. The privilege of getting to encounter even a few beautiful landscapes can create a deep feeling of humility as we realize that our own little lives are but one billionth of a fraction of all that is happening in the universe at any given time.

Whole worlds are out there that we are still learning about. The Webb telescope dominated my newsfeed for months after it began broadcasting, orbiting the sun one million miles away from Earth and capturing breathtaking images from the depths of space. Things never before seen are now visible to our earthly eyes with startling clarity. New spiral galaxies, cosmic cliffs, glittering nebulae, the birthplace of stars—words aren't sufficient to describe the wonders this marvel of technology and human advancement is capturing and sharing with our world. These gorgeous sites have been there for billions of years, and we are just seeing them now for the first time.

Nature keeps me humble, fills me with awe, and blows me away with its beauty. Nature inspires me, and fascinates me, and expands my mind every time I get out there and explore.

Poetic Naturalism

AFTER ADMITTING THAT I NO longer was a Christian, I struggled to know what to call myself instead. My therapist suggested I come up with a positive way to identify now, as opposed to only saying what I wasn't. The hunt for a new label of sorts began.

My friend who has been an atheist for as long as I've known him does not refer to himself as an atheist. For a good reason: he does not wish to identify by what he isn't. We don't do that with any other category. I never identify as non-European or not-a-man or non-vegan. We typically identify by what we *are* or what we do hold value for.

The first label I considered using for myself was a "poetic naturalist," from Sean Carroll's *The Big Picture*. Like I said, that book had a significant impact on me! After teaching me all about emergent truth, Carroll also explained the philosophy of poetic naturalism, which is the belief that the natural, material world is the only world—that there is no spiritual realm at all—but that meaning still exists. No angels, no demons, no ghosts, no Divine Creator lurking in the mist somewhere. He thinks that our human lives are finite, and our consciousness ends when we die, with no afterlife.

I was used to believing in a loving Father up in the sky who counted every hair on my head and cared about what

I did and where I would go when I die. Naturalism initially felt impersonal and cold. But that's where the poetry comes in. Carroll puts it well: "Poetic naturalism emphasizes that there are many ways of talking about the natural world. The fact that the underlying laws of physics are deterministic and impersonal does not mean that at the human level we can't talk about ideas and reasons and goals and purpose and free will."[48] In other words, poetic naturalism allows for a way of viewing the world that is based on scientific fact without throwing out all subjective beauty and morality and concepts that can't be boiled down to scientific theorems. It's a way of admitting to the purposeless nature of the universe while still maintaining that our own individual and collective lives have purpose and meaning.

If science says that, objectively, we are all made of atoms and molecules and that our physical existence has evolved over a long process of trial and error without any divine purpose or plan, that's explaining *what* we are and *how* we got here. But clearly we are more than simply atoms and molecules—we are thinking, feeling creatures capable of love, sarcasm, humor, art, rage, and profound wonder.

Explaining the *what* and the *how* does little when it comes to the *why*. Why does anything exist? Why do we have consciousness? Why are we capable of inflicting love and pain on one another, and does any of it matter? As our shared consciousness expanded and we became capable of asking Big Questions, we created entire philosophies and religions that attempt to get to the meaning of it all. Science is not trying to be religion. Faith and science ask very different questions. Forgiveness, flirting, ritual, morality, mercy, passions, values—none of these things are made of atoms and molecules—and yet they are all completely real and often necessary to living a fulfilling life. We can leave the *what* and the *how* in the scientific realm and continue to discuss, debate, and expand our ideas of *why* and *for what purpose* in our conversations, our philosophies, and our religions.

Poetic naturalism puts things like morality, beauty, and social norms into the emergent truth category discussed earlier, meaning that these are concepts humans have come up with over time to explain and govern our world. In essence, humans made up morality. As I thought about it, it made sense. I could see the path of morality change over time alongside our biological evolution. It used to be morally okay to enslave human beings the world over, but it's now illegal worldwide. It used to be morally okay—and still is in certain cultures—for a grown man to marry a young girl. This is now illegal in most places. Morals change with cultures and with the times because humans not only define morality, we also are constantly redefining it.

Ideals of human beauty are equally fickle and prone to change. The idea of the "perfect woman" has varied wildly over time, going from pale and pudgy in the Victorian age to Twiggy-thin in the '60s to the voluptuous Kardashian ideals of today. In ancient China beautiful women were supposed to have tiny feet, leading to painful foot binding to achieve this impossible goal. Women today wear organ-crushing corsets (I mean, waist trainers) to help accentuate their curves. Point being, physical beauty has meant vastly different things at different times, keeping up with our changing definitions of what beauty means.

Poetic naturalism says that beauty and morality are man-made, evolving, and real. God didn't teach us how to be good and avoid evil—humans have decided and keep deciding what good and evil means ever since we were capable of such thought.

Now, my old Christian red flags flap violently when I think about the idea that we are responsible for defining morality and meaning in our own lives. Isn't there an objective Truth with a capital "T" for right and wrong out there? Humans can't be trusted to define moral behavior ourselves; we'd manipulate the definitions to suit our own purposes immediately! I also doubted our ability to ever achieve true moral behavior on our own without a Divine Savior. If humans are solely responsible for defining and achieving moral behavior, then we are in trouble, right?

But let's assume for a minute that that's the case. If a powerful force called God never actually existed, only the human-made conceptions of god that we created to govern our lives, then humans have evolved and achieved a safer, more just world slowly, so very slowly, on our own all this time. We evolved the ability to create God. We evolved the concept of God into complex, rich systems of thought called religion. Religion evolved to serve a purpose: to unite groups of humans together, to provide structure and purpose for people's lives, to manage behavior.

Religions were a necessary stepping stone on the path of human evolution, and I wonder if the day will come when we evolve beyond religion. When I look at the rest of the natural world, I see evidence of this progression and advancement everywhere. Think of the evolution of plants. What began as slime and ooze, the "primordial soup," slowly evolved into algae, then mosses, then ferns, and eventually trees.

Trees are fascinating. The entire concept of a tree—this gigantic creation of wood, sap, greenery, and fruit, all grown from a small seed—points to the complexity of nature. As a kid, I loved climbing my neighbor's pink dogwood tree in the springtime. I attached myself to a perfectly curved branch, hid in the blossoms, and joined in symbiotic respiration, sharing my carbon dioxide with the tree as it fed my lungs with pure oxygen. The smell was intoxicating, and although I often carted along a book to read up there, I usually ended up staring into the pink canopy and daydreaming until my neighbors came home from work and startled me down from my flowery perch.

Out of all the trees perhaps my favorite is the Giant Redwood. I read a book called *The Wild Trees: A Story of Passion and Daring* by Richard Preston that blew my mind with the intricacy of these humongous beasts. The redwood canopy is so complex and so full of wonderful surprises, "a three-dimensional labyrinth in the air, filled with unknown life."[49] Preston describes men climbing these huge trees, usually in pursuit of the *tallest* tree, but they would often end up making some neat scientific discoveries along the way. They found these little shrimp creatures living in the canopy that had no business living three hundred feet off the forest floor, far from the ocean. There are distinct, new redwood trees that grow up off the thick, horizontal branches of others and huckleberry bushes that live off soil that made its own mysterious way up to the canopy, creating floating gardens in the sky. Enchanting.

I learned from *The Hidden Life of Trees: What They Feel, How They Communicate: Discoveries from a Secret World* by Peter Wohlleben (as well as from watching *The Magic School Bus* again with my kids!) about the complex nature of the forest and how trees use multiple means of communication, including mycelium. These underground fungal networks allow trees to "talk" to each other, via their roots, to let other trees know if dangers are nearby or if they are low on water or certain nutrients—and then they share the necessary nutrients with their fellow trees! Trees are social and cooperative, giving us just one more example of how much we must learn from nature!

Observing the path of evolution in not only the plant but also in the animal world gave me more appreciation for the continual path of advancement. What started off as basic, purely instinctual creatures like worms and insects moved into the more complex but primitive social behaviors of reptiles and eventually advanced into thinking, feeling mammals that demonstrate family bonds and unique cultures. I learned about the intricate social structures and cooperative behavior of wolves, for example, in reading *American Wolf* by Nate Blakeslee. The social hierarchy and interplay of the wolf packs felt like reading a Jane Austen novel: wolves apparently have a culture of deference and respect for the leader and all sorts of nuanced rules for "proper behavior" within the hierarchy!

On a completely different note, my heart was broken by the story of Tahlequah the orca whale carrying her dead calf on her back for *seventeen days* before finally letting her go. The Pacific Northwest orca pods have been struggling with fertility since human interference, by way of dams and fishing, has massively decreased the whales' food supply of salmon. At the time of the story's writing, it had been years since a successful orca birth. Tahlequah had finally birthed a live calf only to have it die within the hour. Her grief was palpable and appeared for all purposes to be on par with human suffering and emotion. Yet I found room for rejoicing with the orcas, too, as Tahlequah successfully gave birth again in 2020![50]

Aside from riding along on this sizeable mammal's emotional journey, I found *When Elephants Weep: The Emotional Lives of Animals* by Jeffrey Moussaieff Masson and Susan McCarthy to be chock-full of examples of emotional animals, both in captivity and in the wild. The authors detail stories of animals displaying high-level emotional behavior such as empathy, altruism, grief, love, shame, and joy.

It became clear to me in reading these accounts that as the animal kingdom has expanded and evolved, all sorts of creatures, humans included, have advanced their species' emotional and social behaviors. The book told of one research study in which scientists tested to see just how many orphaned babies a mother rat would adopt despite needing to cross a pain-inflicting course to get to them. The scientists ran out of babies to use since she kept going after the abandoned little ones! They had to raid neighboring labs to acquire more baby rats for her to save. She apparently would have never stopped hurting herself to save babies unrelated to her, doing nothing for her own gene pool and going against the self-serving *modus operandi* of the evolutionary imperative. Was she demonstrating altruistic compassion? The authors shared how elephants seem to bury and grieve their dead, even traveling far out of their way to revisit old grave sites and pay their respects. Who's to say what is going through their heads? Perhaps some animals do have rituals of grief and mourning that they too have created over time.

I don't know if we can confidently say that any other animal groups have a sense of morality, but *When Elephants Weep* shows how animals do object to hurting each other, seek to protect both their fellow creatures as well as other species—especially if the other animal they are protecting is a baby—and even adopt orphans who are not remotely related to them or their species. Many different types of animals are known to do these things, from rats to chimpanzees. Other animal species seem to have evolved to develop emotions, to create social structures, and to form rituals. Humans evolving to create entire religions seems to fit alongside the development of rest of the natural world.

While sitting around a bonfire during a camping trip in Northern Idaho with my family, I had some time to reflect

on human development. Early human and prehuman creatures would have crouched around campfires identical to
mine. Over millions of years we've gone from grunting
wordless vocalizations to developing entire languages with
complex symbolism and storytelling. We've gone from living in the canopies of trees to building functional dwelling
places on the ground and later beautiful homes and castles.
We've gone from foraging and scavenging to hunting, to
animal husbandry and agriculture, to mega-farms and
supermarkets. We've gone from rock wall art to the works
of Monet, Frida Kahlo, and Basquiat. Early humans would
have looked up at the same star-lit sky as I did then, but by
now we have evolved so far as to build rockets and space
stations. We have *joined* the stars above. Our scientific
advancements have answered many questions that had
been explained by Supernatural Beings in the past. Perhaps
the day will come when we will evolve a new type of system
to bring order to this world after religion.

CONCEIVING OF A WORLD WITHOUT God and learning more
about evolution has caused me to feel a profound sense of
connection to the entire human family. I've come to respect
our distant ancestry as I learned that our species especially
relied on having a community for basic survival. For example, DeSilva, in *First Steps,* explained that while walking on
two feet has certain advantages, a major disadvantage is that
it is more difficult for fetuses to travel through the birth canal.
The pelvis evolved to be narrower when humans switched to

bipedalism. Giving birth became potentially deadly for both mother and baby, so midwives have been necessary from the beginning to ensure the survival of our species.

DeSilva also demonstrates that there is plenty of evidence in the fossil record of prehuman creatures recovering from devastating injuries. That means that early hominins took care of their wounded, slowing down the pack and going out of their way to keep an injured member alive when it was more practical for the group to let it die.[51] When hominins still lived in trees, others would have had to go out of their way to bring the injured creature food and water if it wasn't fit for climbing up and down independently.

My eyes misted up while reading about all this. My ancient ancestors—vulnerable and hunted, never sure of their next meal—survived harsh environments by helping each other. They were more intimately connected with nature and with each other than I will likely ever be with my fellow humans. We are now in an era of technological evolution, scientifically advanced and globally connected and yet often completely ignorant of basic things like where our food comes from and how our clothes are made. I felt awed and grateful for the evolution of empathy and cooperation. Those values evolved to ensure our species' survival, even if we don't use them in a similar capacity today. Even during that prehistoric, immature era of the world— where opinions of fellow tribe members were presumably even more black and white, in and out, member and outsider than they are now—early humans were capable of both compassion and care for one another in their tribe as well as murder and war against the outsiders. We've always contained good and evil within. The starting block was a harsh system of survival-of-the-fittest, eat-or-be-eaten, kill-or-be-killed. We came from a system that encouraged self-ishness and greed for personal survival, and yet we evolved to be compassionate, empathetic, social creatures. How beautiful is that?

Perhaps it is possible, as humanity and consciousness continue to evolve, that we will advance into a peaceful, equitable society. As Martin Luther King Jr. famously said, "The arc of the moral universe is long, but it bends toward justice."[52] We are no longer warring tribes bent on conquer-ing our neighbors (unless your name is Vladimir Putin). No longer is owning another human acceptable in any part of the world (although slavery is not yet *criminalized* every-where—we still have work to do).[53] Steven Pinker wrote a book and gave a wonderful Ted Talk on the many ways humanity has improved, despite how disgusting and evil the world may still seem at times, and on how our society is more highly evolved now than at any previous time in his-tory. [54] Murder rates have gone down, literacy has gone up, and there are more democratic nations than ever before.

Things are objectively improving, at least for the aver-age person, according to the data. However, great inequal-ity remains among the various minorities. Maternal sur-vival rates are three times lower in the U.S.A. for women of color compared to white women.[55] Black men are at least three times more likely (and even more likely in certain communities) to be victims of police violence and murder than white men.[56] Transgender people are frequently forced to limit their presence and code-switch or face higher rates of murder and discrimination.[57] I cannot honestly brag about our human successes until we can apply them to everybody regardless of race, ethnicity, sexuality, gender, or religion. Perhaps our overall statistics are better, but there are individual people still living in dangerous conditions, and they matter. As civil rights activist Fannie Lou Hamer said, "Nobody's free until everybody's free."[58]

As impressed as I am with humans and our general advancement, it can also be hard to look around today and feel hopeful. I'm not naïve to all ugliness still present in the world. I swing between hope and despair regularly. I see wars, child soldiers, sweatshops, addiction and drug problems, racism, homo- and transphobia, environmental abuse, corruption, bigotry of all kinds, constant mass shootings, rape . . . the list goes on. But I also experience great works of art, Lin Manuel Miranda, transcendent moments during live concerts, hugs and kisses from tiny children, delicious meals with great friends, heroes who risk their lives to save strangers and animals, Instagram accounts that are capable of miraculously changing people's political views in a gentle way, food pantries, refugee cities, glorious natural landscapes, and true love.

I am a flaming optimist, but my optimism has taken a beating over the last several years. Optimism used to come naturally to me out of believing that God's love would win out over evil in the end. When I can't believe that a heavenly reward is in their future, watching the suffering of others feels much more depressing. With only flawed humans to rely on for the betterment of society, I find it more challenging to always stay hopeful. But in the wise words of Mr. Rogers' mother, I still try to "look for the helpers. You will always find people who are helping."[59] It's true that humans can completely suck, but their love can also take my breath away. We are all capable of making healthy, caring, and altruistic choices *and* of making selfish, greedy, and apathetic choices. Religious or not, we each have the power to make this world look a little more like heaven or a little more like hell.

I felt comforted thinking that someone was in charge. My sense of justice smiled while envisioning the evil folks of the world getting their just desserts once God finally cleans all this up. It was precisely because of this promised endgame scenario that I found it so daunting to think that the world must be completely random, that things must happen for no cosmic reason at all, and that no one cares. It's scary to think that *we* are in charge. That's so much pressure and responsibility. Perhaps the bravest thing we can do is to own our agency and power in this world, accept the randomness of life and not take it personally, and use whatever meager influence we hold to do our part to turn this place into heaven on Earth.

ON LABOR DAY WEEKEND THIRTEEN years ago, my friends and I went camping in Glacier National Park. It was my second trip to the park after moving to Spokane, and I was hypnotized by its beauty. Dramatic, sheer rock faces on towering, snow-covered mountains dominate the landscape. Evergreens poke the sky as far as the eye can see. Alpine wildflowers, hoary marmots, mountain goats, snow-melt rivers, and cascading waterfalls are hidden around every corner. There are forests and meadows and lakes and, of course, glaciers (for a little while longer, anyway). The place is breathtaking, and I hope to return as often as possible.

On this trip we wanted to hike to Iceberg Lake on a trail that was recommended to me by several trusted outdoorsy friends. However, that trail had closed for the weekend due to prolific bear activity in the area. Sure enough, as we drove into the Many Glacier region of the northeast corner of the park, we encountered a traffic jam as people pulled off the road to gaze down the hillside and watch two grizzly bears forage for late-summer berries. We had no qualms about bypassing that particular hike, knowing we would be back in the future to make another—safer—attempt.

We inquired at the Many Glacier Lodge to find a comparable trail for the day, asking one of the strapping bellboys sporting the traditional lederhosen uniform (the women were all in GNP polos and khakis, and we could not figure why only the men had to wear those goofy, traditional outfits). He recommended the Grinnell Glacier Overlook trail, about a twelve-mile round trip.

So we set out, our packs filled with rain jackets, bagged lunches, trail mix, water, and chocolate. I had advised the girls to pack mittens and hats as well, as it can snow in September in the park.

We felt prepared and hit the trail chatting and singing, behaving as noisily as possible to scare away any grizzly neighbors. We cracked ourselves up practicing "scary bear faces" in the event we needed to frighten a grizzly, and our spirits were high. As we began to gain some elevation and hiked our way into a misty cloud, we confidently pulled out our rain gear and trudged on. The mist was thick and quickly morphed into a true drizzle, and the mountain peaks in the distance were shrouded in foreboding cloud cover. Traditionally I am a sunshine-and-blue-skies kind of girl, happiest when bombarded with golden rays. This place was so beautiful, however, that even in the clouds and rain, I could scarcely keep from gasping and exclaiming about the lovely scene we were privy to. The gray skies made the pines and firs turn a deeper shade of green, and the dark outline of storm clouds behind the snow-covered peaks was striking.

At one point, just as we reached an overlook above Grinnell Lake, the sun broke out from behind the clouds for several minutes to illuminate the lake in the purest tones of teal and turquoise that I had ever beheld in nature. It was a truly majestic moment. We stood—panting, dripping—in silence to appreciate the scene before us. Wisps of cloud played in front of the sun, causing the surface of the water to morph and change colors like a giant prism.

Content to stay and stare forever, we reluctantly pushed up and on as the cold mountain air began to seep through our damp clothes. About a mile or two further up the trail, we noticed that the drizzle had taken on a thicker quality. In fact, the drops hitting my jacket were noticeably white.

We were now hiking in the snow! Not to be easily deterred, we donned our winter wear and bravely continued. Soon we saw familiar faces approaching—a couple that had passed us earlier had now turned back, put off by the September snow. We stopped and conferred for a moment, but we decided that the glacial overlook would be worth the cold and kept going.

The next couple we encountered was a bit older—slightly older than most of our parents—and voiced deep concern for our group. The snow was falling more densely, with a meaner bite in the air, and our gear was losing the battle to keep our body heat away from the selfish grasp of the wind. Apparently several miles were left to reach the end of the trail, and this couple made it clear that they advised us to turn tail and hike back down.

We politely thanked them for their opinion and—now with our pride challenged and unwilling to back down—forged ahead. The trail had risen at least fifteen hundred feet by then, and the sights we saw were breathtaking. We were hiking in a snow globe. The trail skirted a sheer rock face with frigid water splashing down its surface in a joyful dance with gravity. Plants and flowers received a dusting of powdered sugar as the snow began to accumulate. We stopped under a rocky overhang to eat our lunches in peace from the onslaught of snow, and as our body temperatures cooled and blood flow slowed, we made the difficult decision to turn back.

Making our way back down the trail, we enjoyed an entirely new landscape. Our trail was now snow-covered for the first couple of return miles, and we faced the opposite direction, seeing the mountains that had been to our backs previously. As we reached the bottom of the mountain and hiked alongside Lake Josephine, the sun broke out once again and warmed our rain-and-snow-soaked faces. Our trailhead had begun near the entrance to the Many Glacier Lodge, so we decided to take our sopping selves inside to be warmed by the radiators and steaming mugs of chai lattes.

Even sitting in the basement of the lodge was a beatific experience. We were in no rush to return to our wet, cold tent. We planted ourselves in front of the floor-to-ceiling windows—hiking boots laid out on radiators to dry, feet propped on comfy chairs, journals and books in hand—and enjoyed the peaceful scene for several hours. My friend Andrea found a piano in the basement and treated us all to the perfect soundtrack for our day. High above the Swift-current Lake and mountain peaks, the sun and clouds continued to duke it out in an aerial display more visually entertaining than any movie I had ever seen.

Looking back on our day, I could only laugh. Getting snowed on in late summer, singing every camp song in the book to scare away roaming grizzlies, taking over the basement of the lodge to thaw out and dry our soaked goods—nothing about that day was predictable or expected, and it turned out better than any of us could have planned. In fact, particularly because our plans went awry, the day was made more memorable.

It reminded me of when I used to want to be a marine biologist, mainly because of the early childhood influence of *Free Willy*. I even went on a college visit during high school to investigate that school's partnership program with Hawaii Pacific University. I had envisioned a sun-soaked, tropical plan for my life that involved going to school in Wisconsin for two years before transferring to HPU to complete my degree and play in the ocean all day. My parents saw the folly in my thinking and realized that being a marine biologist was a far way off from my day-dreams. They gently goaded the marine biology department chair to emphasize how much lab work I'd be getting into, and my bubble quickly popped.

However, that same college had recently developed a physical therapy program, and our tour guide made several references to it while walking around the campus. My parents then subtly mentioned how well-suited I was to physical therapy and made a few comments about how great that career could be for my temperament and desired life-style. I was convinced. Because of that innocent manipulation, my whole life changed.

Because of one friend's road trip, I ended up moving out to Spokane, Washington, after graduating from Marquette.

Because of another friend's brother's online dating experience, I ended up meeting my husband.

Life is random, and the most bizarre things can end up profoundly changing your life. If things had randomly gone another way, my life could be drastically different. How wonderful.

Nature is unpredictable and fickle. While in the out-doors, it's hard to get too comfortable or stay stagnant too long, as things can quickly change course like a storm blowing over the Continental Divide. Nature has taught me how to adapt, how to be flexible, and how to persevere in the face of unexpected challenges. That is coming in quite handy now while I adapt to this massive spiritual upheaval. And for that, I am deeply grateful.

Christian Atheist

WHILE STILL THINKING ABOUT HOW to identify myself after my departure from Christianity, I listened to Mike McHargue discuss his spiritual journey on a podcast called *Flightless Bird* with David Farrier. I was familiar with Mike from the podcast world and from reading his second book, *You're a Miracle (and a Pain in the Ass): Embracing the Emotions, Habits, and Mystery That Make You You.* McHargue grew up Southern Baptist, served as a deacon in his church, became an atheist for several years, and then had a mystical experience that reintroduced him to the faith, this time in the style of my beloved Madeleine L'Engle with Christian mysticism. McHargue is scientifically minded (known as "Science Mike" when he spoke on *The Liturgists* podcast). He had a strange experience that involved being enveloped in light and feeling an overwhelming sense of profound peace and love. He immediately thought he had a brain tumor. When no tumor was revealed, he inferred that there must be something else out there, something yet unexplained, and he has no problem using the language of his youth and referring to that thing as God.[60]

In the podcast, McHargue also discussed a fascinating scientific experiment in which patients who were suffering from seizure disorders had a part of their brains called the *corpus callosum* cut and completely severed.[61] The *corpus callosum* is the bridge between the left and right hemispheres of the brain. Although all brain tissue can learn to perform all tasks of the brain, there are sections that become dedicated to certain tasks, so we talk about the left hemisphere of the brain processing language and the right hemisphere dealing with visual, spatial-awareness information.

Folks who had their *corpus callosum* cut, then, basically had *two* brains that were not in communication with each other. Experiments were enacted by communicating with the left or the right brain separately. The left brain could respond to questions via talking since the left hemisphere controls speech, and the right brain would use the left hand (the right brain controls the left side of the body) to write out answers. People were asked questions like, "Do you have a crush on the test administrator?" Some answered "No" orally with their left brain, but their right brain spelled out "Yes!" One subject was asked if they believed in God, and they answered both yes and no via their two different brains. What?!

This is fascinating to me: the idea that we contain paradox and controversy in our very cells, in the tissues of our brains. It's even more evidence against seeing the world through that definitive, black-and-white lens. Things are never so simple as two opposing choices; there is always a middle zone: black, white, *and* gray; male, female, *and* intersex and non-binary; night, day, *and* dusk and dawn; water, land, *and* marshes, bogs, bayous, *and* shores; zeros, ones *and* fractions; good, evil, *and* the flawed hero or merciful bad guy; gay, straight, *and* bisexual, asexual, and more. Paradox abounds. McHargue has landed in this same place, saying he believes in God about three out of ten days, and the other seven days, he is an atheist. He does still identify as Christian.

I am not on the same page as Mike, believing in God some of the time but not all the time. At this point in my life, I think there isn't a god or Higher Being out there 100% of the time. My renouncement of God is too fresh, and a major reason I felt relief at my unbelief was the end of the cognitive dissonance I experienced for so long. I don't think of the universe as a god-substitute, somehow working with will and intention to bring people and opportunities our way. I truly believe that no one is in charge anywhere out there in the background of our lives.

Yet I considered the label "Christian atheist" after listening to Mike, not because I do and don't believe in God, but because I feel like I am an atheistic cultural Christian, akin to a secular Jewish person. Because I continue to be culturally involved in Christianity while I attend church with my family and socialize with predominantly religious friends. I still enjoy discussing (picking apart) the Bible, and I enjoy debating spiritual theories. I like this approach because as I laid out earlier, Christianity created me. The foundation of my life was centered around Christ. It greatly contributed (for better or for worse) to so much of my essence—my values, my morality, my language, my behavior, my tastes, my sexuality, my life choices.

I *am* a Christian in my cells because I was raised so deeply in the faith and molded by it. Christianese is my first spiritual language, infused into the air I breathed for over thirty years. When someone I know is going through a hard time now, I still tell them that I am praying for them. And I mean it—I am no longer praying *to God*, but I am praying *for them* and am sending love, hope, peace, and good thoughts their way. The term "prayer" still conveys my intention, namely that they are in my heart and I am concerned for and invested in their well-being.

Christian words and phrases are still quick to leap off my tongue, and I catch myself humming old church songs on occasion. Biblical concepts and stories I long ago memorized still come to mind at appropriate times. I maintain all the knowledge I've acquired over the decades about the Bible, the ancient Hebrews, life during Roman-occupied Jerusalem, and the kingdom of God. And yet, currently, I do not think that there is a Supernatural Being somewhere who created all this on purpose.

"Christian atheist" is a confusing term to say, which I also enjoy. Throwing out the word *Christian* these days conjures up all different kinds of images and ideas. For some, Christians are kind, loving people with strong morals who believe in forgiveness, mercy, service, and love. For others, Christians are folks who believe that gay people are doomed to hell, that science is full of lies, and that women don't deserve a public voice or control over their own bodies. Some Christians identify as such but only attend church once or twice a year, typically at Easter and Christmas.

Some never go to church, believing that they can live out their faith in isolation without being surrounded by community. Others are at church up to three times a week or even attend daily Mass.

Some Christians swear; others believe a real Christian would never cuss. Some Christians drink; some are alcoholics, and some are teetotalers. Many Christians have sex outside of marriage; others think that is completely forbidden. Some Christians are queer; other Christians believe being anywhere on the LGBTQIA scale is going against God's creation and is a roadblock to salvation. Some Christians believe Christ's saying that it is harder for a rich man to enter heaven than a camel go through the eye of a needle[62] and therefore live modest lives or even take a vow of poverty, while others believe in the prosperity gospel and that God will bless them with good health and material wealth if they're well-behaved. Some Christians think speaking in tongues is a litmus test for true believers; others would never attempt such a thing. Some Christians think that the current translation of the Bible they happen to be reading is God's verbatim truth, to be followed exactly as the English words read on the paper; others believe that the Bible is a complex, multi-stylistic scholarly document that deserves intense study in its original languages with a heavy dose of context.

Identifying as a Christian these days is convoluted and often requires clarification anyway. So many different beliefs and lifestyles, all under the same banner. Does anyone have it right?

But saying that I am a Christian atheist *really* makes people pause. Those two concepts seem to be in direct opposition to each other! But that very thing provides me with an avenue to spit in the binary's face. It invites a conversation. It allows me to explain that I was raised as a Christian and formed by the faith but that I now believe that the physical world is all there is. Yet I retain much of the culture of Christianity without submitting to the entire belief system.

I like the term "Christian atheist" for leaning into the mystery and the paradox of it all, for paying homage to my roots while acknowledging my current state of belief, and for making people think. But perhaps I'm overcomplicated it.

I AM A WATER GIRL at heart. I grew up in Crystal Lake, Illinois, and spent nearly every day of every summer in the lake. I would splash around and pretend to be Ariel from *The Little Mermaid* with my friends for hours until we had perfected the scene where she bursts out of the waves singing "Part of Your World!" I grew up idolizing the lifeguards and later became one myself. I got paid to sit and watch the sun set over the western shore of Crystal Lake all during high school.

Lakes are gathering places. Families bring picnics and camp out for the day on the beach, getting together to let the kids play while parents lie in the sun and mess with the grill. In the wild, animals of all sizes draw near lakes to quench their thirst. Lakes foster community and fellowship.

The summer camp I attended when I was eleven years old had a small lake with one very special feature—The Blob. The Blob was a giant air pillow that sat on top of the water. The camp had made a tall, wooden tower for campers to climb up, with a platform at the top to jump off and land on one end of The Blob. The camper perched at the other end would be launched into the air from the impact, flying high before hitting the water with a splash.

Camp was a feral place, but there were some rules. One major rule was the size difference allowed between jumpers on The Blob. Whoever jumped to launch a camper off The Blob could not be more than twenty pounds heavier; otherwise, the launched camper would fly too high in the air and risk getting injured on their reentry into the lake.

My counselor was cool. She was a young college student with a strong, muscular body, and I wanted her to launch me. She agreed to a super stealthy maneuver we devised (that I'm sure the lifeguard on duty *totally* didn't notice) to switch places with the person who was supposed to jump behind me after she bailed out at the top, claiming to be too scared to jump at the last minute. My tiny four-foot eight-inch, eighty-pound frame was tingling with excitement, perched on the far edge of The Blob, when suddenly I went *flying*.

I flew so high into the air that I had ample time to realize that I was not yet beginning my descent. I kept going up and up before gravity finally took over and ripped me, screaming, back to the surface of the water while leaving my stomach dangling up above in midair. Despite wearing a life jacket, I went so far under the surface as to feel seaweed at the bottom of the lake. In fact, a piece of sea-weed snaked itself around one of my legs, twining itself into a tight hold that caused a moment of panic. Thankfully, the pull of the life jacket was strong enough to overcome the seaweed's grip, and I popped back up to the surface like a champagne cork.

Lakes are fun.

Although I would take a lake over the ocean most days, there is also something very alluring about the sea. The ocean feels like the last frontier—vast and primal. It is fickle and mysterious, potentially peaceful and lethal all in the same breath. When I think of the ocean and all its beauty—tropical islands, gargantuan wildlife, colorful reefs—and all its risks—rip tides, deadly creatures, tsunamis—I feel a complex emotion of fear mixed with awe, respect, and wonder.

When I was ten, my dad had a sales contract with a company in California and managed to take my mom, my brother, and me along on the trip. He had to do some work while we were there, but he was able to get away enough to take us all to Disneyland and SeaWorld. On a day that he couldn't join us, my mom decided to adventure out without him and took my brother and me to Newport Beach. The weather was overcast but warm enough to swim, and we didn't realize that there was a large storm brewing out at sea that affected the swell in ways we were not skilled at reading.

I can still feel the terrifying sensation of standing in ankle-deep water at the edge of the ocean as a huge wave crashed on the shore, immediately submerging me up to my chest and then sucking me out as the wave withdrew. I felt perfectly safe one minute, standing far back on shore at the tiniest edge of the waterline, and in the next instant I felt abject terror when I thought I was getting pulled out to sea. I was able to dig my heels into the sand and narrowly avoid getting swept away.

Thankfully my mom was paying close attention and realized that no one else was swimming and quickly called it a day. We ate our picnic on the sandy shore and watched the waves crash from afar.

If lakes cause me to think of fun and recreation and oceans of power and awe, then rivers demonstrate that life is ever-changing and a constant journey. The Spokane River runs right through the city and even has a series of rapids and waterfalls observable from bridges crisscrossing through downtown. When I initially moved here from the Midwest, I had an entire month of downtime before I started my job. I had already passed my physical therapy board exam and secured a job with a large healthcare company that was slow to onboard me. My roommate was studying for her board exam full-time and started working before I did, so I had a lot of time on my own to explore and learn about my new home. I spent several hours in Riverfront Park downtown reading a book, people-watching, and studying the river as it raced by.

I had landed in Spokane after years of traveling all around Maine, Northeastern Canada, and Arizona while completing my physical therapy clinicals with side trips to

Yellowstone, Texas, Minnesota, and Indiana in between school events. When I wrapped up my last clinical in Phoenix, I drove back to Milwaukee, attended my graduation ceremony, moved back home for a couple of weeks, had one last camping trip in the Midwest with some friends from home, and then moved out to Spokane. A whirlwind of activity and adventure brought me to my new home. Just like life, rivers rush ahead without a pause. They may speed up, slow down, and even change course, but they constantly push forward.

Having specific experiences in nature has taught me a lot about myself and the world, particularly my interactions around water. I love the water. I enjoy swimming in it, playing on it, and drinking it after an exhausting workout or a long day's hike. I love to watch it fall down a cliff face, listen to it gently lap on a lakeshore, or hear it roar and crash where the ocean meets the earth for hours on end. I was on the swim team in high school, and I never tired of diving into the pool, reveling in the feeling of it on my skin, streaming through my hair as my body blasted through its depths.

Water is so intriguing because of all the various forms it can take. It's the master of disguise: lakes, oceans, rivers, puddles, clouds, fog, icicles, snow, cascading waterfalls, glassy ponds, prismatic glints of diamond splashed into the sun-filled air, the white foam in the wake of a motorboat, the whirling eddies behind the kayak's paddle.

If water can take on any form and style imaginable, I can be a cultural Christian who is also an atheist. I can be a poetic naturalist who was formed by Christianity and is agnostic about the greatest mysteries of life. I can doubt the existence of God while wishing they were real. I can believe that my existence will end with my physical death and hope for an afterlife in heaven in the same breath. Nature can exist in many phases and forms, and I am a part of nature. Nature has given me permission to be myself without boundaries, without labels, without limits.

Agnostic

AN AGNOSTIC IS "A PERSON who holds the view that any ultimate reality (such as God) is unknown and probably unknowable; broadly: one who is not committed to believing in either the existence or the nonexistence of God or a god."[63] While I'm fairly convinced that a god of any sort isn't fundamentally real, I am not so cocky as to believe that I can truly know anything about why any of this is here or what happens after we die.

Unexplainable things happen that I don't know how to handle. Near-death experiences are a solid example of something happening outside the explanation of science. Although there is variation in every NDE, the list of commonalities is uncanny: seeing a bright light, seeing a loved one, watching a review of one's life, a heightened sense of reality or an out-of-body experience. This usually occurs when the person is clinically dead and not apparently conscious.

After Catherine Wolff touched on NDEs in her book *Beyond*, I dug deeper and checked out *After: A Doctor Explores What Near-Death Experiences Reveal about Life and Beyond* by Bruce Greyson, MD. Dr. Greyson has dedicated much of his life to robust and rigorous scientific study of this phenomenon. He is not personally convinced one way or another about the reality of an afterlife and appears to be truly objective in his research.

There are countless persons worldwide who have experienced inexplicable events during a close brush with death. For instance, they might see deceased relatives that they'd never met but would later identify in family photos. They might have out-of-body experiences such as traveling around the hospital where they were dying and seeing events take place in other rooms that they should not have been able to accurately describe. They may encounter a "spirit guide" instructing them to inform a perfect stranger of the need to get checked out for cancer, which indeed would later turn out to be present in the stranger's body. There are no easy explanations for these events. NDEs currently operate outside our models of science, much like the quantum world operates outside of Newton's laws of physics.

Strange things happen, like Mike McHargue's experience with the enveloping light mentioned a few chapters ago. My mom is infamous for her outlandish stories in which she should have died but didn't. As a child, she rolled out of a moving car on a busy road in her ballet tutu (apparently children never wore seatbelts in the '50s) and safely ran to the side of the road without a scratch. During a cross-country road trip with a friend, her car flipped over on the side of the highway. They were rescued by a passing motorcycle gang that came out of nowhere and couldn't be seen leaving the scene after they calmed down and looked around to thank their saviors—despite the endless stretch of flat highway.

The story of hers that makes me pause the most happened when she was on a camping trip with her family as a child. She had befriended the childless couple in the cabin across from hers, and one day they offered to take her out for ice cream. She asked her parents if she could go and was given the okay, but as she walked toward their car, she heard a deep, male voice say, "No!" She flipped around to whine at her dad and begged him to change his mind, and he was confused, puzzled by her complaints—because he hadn't said anything. She hesitated, then turned back to get in the car when she heard the voice again: "No!" She became uneasy and decided not to go get ice cream. The couple left and strangely never returned to the campsite after that. It's a story my grandma never liked to talk about, and one that is shrouded in mystery.

Did my mom really hear a voice? Whose? God's? Her own inner-knowing or subconscious?

I experienced something strange myself while hiking in the Superstition Mountains near Phoenix, Arizona, where I spent two months in the spring of 2010 for a clinical rotation. I knew no one there, so when I was off work, I spent a lot of time hiking on my own through the desert. This would not have been too enjoyable during the months of July or August, but in March and April I was in a sandy heaven. Armed with several water bottles and sunscreen, I hit the trails nearly every weekend and often after a long day of work.

New to that landscape, I was awed by the height of the saguaro cacti. Too curious for my own good, I impaled my

Nalgene water bottle (I thought they were unbreakable!) on a tough cactus spine while testing to see how strong they were. There was not a lot of wildlife, although little geckos and birds flitted around, and I was surprised by the amount and diversity of wildflowers along the way. Bright yellow, orange, and magenta littered the path. My favorite flower was the cactus blossom. The bright pink shocked my eyes and attracted my attention from far away.

Phoenix is a busy city, and many of the hiking trails were overcrowded, especially those closest to downtown where I would go after work. Weekends were the best time to get away from the hustle and bustle; I got a better feel for the desert then.

My favorite hike in Arizona was the Boulder Canyon Trail in the Superstition Mountain Range east of the city. The drive to the hike alone was worth the trip. Pulling off Highway 60, I quickly entered the mountains, and my trusty old Buick LeSabre, Berta Mae, had fun powering up the steep grades. I was compelled to stop several times to take pictures from the side of the road. As I rounded the final bend in the road, my eyes were greeted with a beautiful sight—water! The blue waters of Canyon Lake were a balm to my dry eyes after seeing so much beige, tan, and umber.

I found my trailhead and set out for the day, planning to do a sixteen-mile loop with a hiking book on loan from my clinical instructor to guide the way. The trail was nearly deserted except for a few pokey couples ambling along at the beginning, admiring the spring blossoms. Less than a mile down the path I was the only human in sight.

The horizon was a sight to behold. After summiting the first hill, I peered down into La Barge Canyon filled with cacti, shrubbery, bright yellow flowers, and rocks galore. Off in the distance Weaver's Needle boldly pierced the sky. The only shade came from adequately sized boulders or particularly thick cacti. There was a creek running along the valley floor that offered a gentle soundtrack when I finally trekked within earshot.

The guide book recommended leaving the trail and hopping from boulder to boulder up the creek bed for several miles to get to a cool, blue swimming hole. As the temperature approached 95°F, my main objective for the day became taking a dip in this wilderness oasis. After hiking down into the canyon, I started up the creek bed. The going became tough, and my progress significantly slowed. Normally I liked to maintain a decent pace to really get my heart rate up, but here I did not mind casually leaping from rock to rock, admiring the views and the cool breeze coming up off the water. I scaled a tall boulder with a shady spot at the top from the nearby cliff to eat my sack lunch of a peanut butter and honey sandwich, warm grapes, and melty chocolate.

While relaxing a bit and enjoying my lunch on the rock, I stopped to think of where I was and what I was doing. The woman I was staying with in Phoenix had no idea where I had gone that day since she was a night-shift nurse, and we frequently passed like ships in the night. No one knew where I was—I had not seen another person since those few couples at the start of the trail, and I was certain that they would not make it this far; not to mention the fact that I had now left the trail and was miles off in the middle of the rocky wilderness.

Too often (as my mother would certainly lament) I am too brave and rash for my own good and end up placing myself in some sticky situations. The risks were plentiful—rattlesnakes were common at that time of year, and in fact, I had just treated a patient at the hospital with a rattlesnake bite. I could have sprained an ankle or encountered a fellow mountain adventurer with less than pure intentions. While chewing my food, I sensed—I hesitate to say "heard" although it seemed nearly audible—a voice say, "Go back."

It was so real. The words felt telepathically implanted in my brain. I was freaked out enough to turn around and bounce back to the trail. Who knows if anything bad would have happened had I continued? I'll never know. Maybe it's possible that a Divine Being protected me from harm. It is also possible that my subconscious realized the risk I was taking and reached out from deep within my brain in an act of self-preservation.

BEYOND MIRACULOUS RESCUES, INEXPLICABLE STORIES, and hearing words on the wind, there is still the perplexing fact that science does not know how all this truly started—why this universe even exists. The initiation of the Big Bang, which is less of an event and more like a "label for a moment in time that we currently don't understand,"[64] makes no sense. The Big Bang helps to explain observed phenomena like cosmic background radiation and tries to make sense of what is objectively *here*, but its own existence is a mystery.

What was going on before the Big Bang? Was there a *before*? Did someone or something set it off, and if so, where did *that* thing come from? *Why* did the Big Bang happen? Where did it get all that dense material to explode? Why does the universe have governing laws and all the different kinds of materials it's full of? There is no reason for any of this to exist—and yet here we are.

Mysteries abound.

I strive to remain humble and open to new information. If we suddenly received proof that intelligent alien life had seeded the universe with its DNA and has been rooting for our progress from afar, I would rejoice. If we got proof of a spiritual realm in which a loving Creator fashioned this world with us in mind, fan-damn-tastic! If we found out that we are all dreaming this entire existence and are plugged into a Matrix-like computer . . . okay?

Of course I wish that there was a purpose to all this and that evil will one day be conquered and that love will prevail, but I simply do not know. I know that's where "faith" comes in, but for now, there is too much evidence to the contrary for me to support that story. For me it would be wishful thinking rather than faith to believe that.

I do not know, and that is okay.

THE SUMMER OF 2009 LIVES in my mind as an unforgettable adventure of the most epic proportions. My friend Kari and I had signed up together to do our summer clinical rotation in Presque Isle, Maine. This tiny town in the northeast corner of the state stole a piece of my heart, and to this day I think about some of the wonderful people I met out there. The rotation was ten weeks long, and it landed smack-dab in the middle of the summer. In addition, we had five weeks of freedom before starting our last year of PT school, so we took two weeks to drive out there and three to return, putting 5,500 miles on Kari's car while stopping to visit friends and sightsee along the way.

With stopovers in Pennsylvania, Boston, Portland, Camden, Mt. Katahdin, Quebec City, Fredericksburg, Kouchibouguac National Park (the best-named park I've ever beheld), Prince Edward Island, Halifax, Bar Harbor, the Green Mountains of Vermont, Buffalo, and Kalamazoo, we saw much of the glory that southeastern Canada and the northeastern U.S.A. have to offer. Although it is impossible to pick a favorite spot among all the places we visited, if forced, I would have to say that Nova Scotia's coast was my favorite: rugged, rocky, and outlined with evergreens. Fog shrouded the edge of the sea in mystery.

Kari and I spent most of our time out in nature, exploring by feet or by kayak, roughing it and camping in each location, and eating instant oatmeal every single morning while trying to conserve our meager, grad-school-depleted funds. In Halifax, we enjoyed mixing it up and booked a stay in a hostel, went out to eat at nice restaurants, and enjoyed more urban explorations during their annual Busker Festival and while catching a play from "Shakespeare by the

Sea." Despite the fun to be had in the city, we couldn't resist a day of driving along the coast and into the country.

Cruising along Canadian Highway 333 and around the edge of St. Margaret's Bay was a dream. We pulled out of the bustling city and into a parallel universe of fog horns, oversized wool sweaters, fishermen, and the sea. Obscured by the fog, the road didn't reveal what was coming until it was fifty yards in front of us. This made driving a little precarious and that much more exciting.

We stopped in the small town of Peggy's Cove where a scenic lighthouse dominated the landscape and half of the buildings in town were art boutiques. The fog morphed into outright rain, so we made a quick dash onto the rocks for umbrella-screened photos of the lighthouse before running into the Sou'wester Restaurant & Gift Shop to warm up with mugs of coffee.

When the weather cleared, we ventured back outside and roamed the rocky shore some more before exploring the local shops. The collections were well out of our price range, but we had fun pretending we were actual customers and enjoyed the beautiful works of art. Given the town's population of less than fifty, we quickly saw all there was to see and got back in our car to continue exploring.

The highway hugged the edge of the bay and brought us through several other small art towns. We met a friendly hammock-maker who gave us a quick demo of his craft. We met a husband-and-wife team who ran their gallery out of their front yard shop and made all their works of art on-site. They each had their own distinctive style, yet their loving relationship was plainly portrayed throughout their works.

We had parked the car in the residential neighborhood of this latest gallery, and as we wandered back to the car, I spied a cozy scene on the shore of this little inlet. Adirondack chairs, a bonfire pit, and an end table within easy reach—complete with wine glass and coffee mug rings. A view of the sailboat-filled bay. Fog obscured the further edges of the inlet and streamed through the branches of a nearby rose bush. Making myself comfortable in the Adirondack, I relaxed into this snug scene, and my mind was drawn to the fog.

I have a thing for weather. Growing up on the outskirts of tornado alley, my family experienced major storms every summer. I know the exact, eerie shade of green that the sky turns during tornado weather. Between tornado warnings, fantastic lightning and thunderstorms, blistering heat and humidity, and frigid winters that buried us under feet of snow, I have a deep respect for weather and the various moods it could create within me. Fog has always been mysterious, obscuring the surroundings and reaching densities so thick it could be possible to walk right off a cliff without warning.

Meditating on the fog, I appreciated the unknowable path of my life. Metaphorical fog often descends at crossroads in my life when my future is uncertain and a decision must be made. As much as I am a planner and attempt to control my fate, I find it ultimately undeniable—especially in the face of natural disasters, wild weather, and global pandemics—that our lives are randomly blown about by the wind. We cannot accurately predict too far down the path of life and must wade through the fog to discover what is coming up next.

The fog reminds me that I cannot control everything. And that can be beautiful, especially when I do my best to forge ahead and adapt as I go.

Divine

So HERE I WAS, WALKING through the world after announcing that I no longer believed in God, and my snarky side was tickled to notice that shortly after I was brave enough to say the words aloud, things in my personal life took a massive turn for the better.

My family struggled during the pandemic after I was laid off from my job in March 2020. I had been the stable breadwinner in our family as my husband is self-employed. His income was unpredictable and unreliable, and he struggled with the sudden pressure of supporting our family.

I was floundering and didn't know how to proceed when *no one* in my community was hiring in my niche of outpatient, orthopedic physical therapy. Mentally I went rapid-fire through the options without focus: lean into being a stay-at-home mom, try to be self-employed as a PT, never work as a PT ever again, go back to school for mental health counseling, or lean into activism and look for a job in racial reconciliation or environmental conservation. I became lost in a whirlwind of confusion to the point that I needed professional guidance from a therapist.

The therapist provided the clarity I needed, and he encouraged me to pursue the option that he sensed I was the most serious about. I ultimately ended up opening my own PT clinic in August 2020 to see some patients and keep my license active. I had never planned on owning my own clinic—was on the record with my husband that I never *wanted* to run my own clinic—but with the safety blanket of unemployment extended to newly self-employed folks during the Crazy Times, it seemed like a good time to try. Though I had some meager success during my first year of operation, I was not pulling in nearly the money I had been while working for someone else. Our financial situation was the worst it had ever been.

Towards the end of 2021 we lost our free childcare (a generous cousin who had been watching our kids on her one day off a week while I tried to get the clinic going), *and* I lost the affordable location that I had been sharing with an acupuncturist as she decided to leave when our lease expired. I could not find anywhere to go that wouldn't be at least double the rent, and I wasn't pulling in a consistent caseload to handle higher expenses like that.

My husband landed in the ER with mysterious ailments as the stress from our finances and his own career began to manifest physically. Things were not looking good.

During all that time, I was wrestling with these questions about God, and sometime in mid-2021, I landed in my atheistic position. When all the barriers to continuing my clinic popped up, I decided to see if folks were hiring again and ultimately took a job in a new area of physical therapy, working with the elderly in an assisted living facility. I was offered the job immediately after my interview despite having no experience in that arena, and the pay was markedly higher than I had been making at my pre-self-employed job, with benefits. I also quickly inherited thirty new grandmas; the old ladies I primarily treat now are sweet and encouraging and think I'm the greatest thing ever. I ride my bike to work and have been told on numerous occasions to be careful going home because "I worry aboutcha."

Not only are my new grandmas sweet, but they are fascinating. One of my patients was a real-life Rosie the Riveter! I've met people who met President Reagan and Mother Theresa. Many of them remember details about Pearl Harbor or VE Day. Most of my patients were born during the Great Depression. Some of them lived without indoor plumbing or electricity. They were born before humans had landed on the moon or invented computers, let alone the internet. I love asking these people questions and hearing their interesting perspectives on life.

My new boss is supportive of families and respects the work/life balance. He was willing to work my schedule around the days and hours that made the most sense for my family, and, conveniently, the hours the old folks want to be seen are basically school hours. They refuse to be treated any earlier than 8:30 a.m., and they need to start getting ready for dinner by 4:00 p.m., which maps nicely to the hours when we need to drop off and pick up our kids from school.

By February 2022, I felt relieved, at peace, and content in my new job.

We even found a distant relative to hire who was thrilled with the opportunity to watch our kids and is committed to and flexible with our needs—and she also generously cleans my house while I'm gone! A true unicorn of childcare. She doesn't have children of her own and was longing for a way to fulfill her nurturing cravings. I had previously used professional nannies but with horrible luck; we went through three nannies in three months. Searching, interviewing, and calling references made that whole endeavor a part-time job in and of itself. Knowing we have a family member committing to us for the long haul and who truly loves our kids is a massive relief.

My husband's job had several long-lasting projects that finally wrapped up, providing us with several nice paychecks. It felt like we had some money to play with again and could loosen the straps on our tight budget. We even pulled off a trip to Hawaii in May 2022 for our ten-year anniversary, leaving the kids home with grandparents.

To top it all off, I started getting free time to myself in the mornings on the days I was home as both my kids were now enrolled in preschool. Glorious free time, time to write! I finally made an appointment (during my new free time) with a dermatologist to clear up the chronic acne I've dealt with all my life. After letting my hair grow out to its natural, darker color during the pandemic, I realized that I am happiest as a blond and lightened it back up again (more free time fun). I got a few new piercings (a free time adventure) that spark joy every day. Cosmetically, financially, mentally, and emotionally, life was good. I felt secure, content, and at peace.

If there was a god out there, they certainly weren't pun-
ishing me for my extreme level of doubting their existence.

ONE EVENING I WAS DRIVING home from work as the sun
was setting. The atmosphere felt velvety soft, and it looked
as if the air itself turned yellow with the colors of the setting sun. The clouds, the leaves on the trees, and even the
ugly rooftops of the passing houses glowed with a yellow
luminescence as if lit from within. As I was soaking up the
beautiful moment, I realized that in the past, I would have
prayed and praised God for their beautiful creation. I
started to cry, sad that I no longer believed that I had a god
to share this moment with. But then I realized that the sunset was still beautiful. I could appreciate the beauty all on
its own without needing anyone to thank.

I continue to grieve the loss of God in my life, even as I
move forward.

I'VE DECIDED TO NOT MAKE my mind up about anything
spiritual. The label I ultimately landed on is an atheistic
agnostic, although I like to bounce between all my options
depending on the situation. I don't believe that a Higher
Being exists, but I don't claim to know with any level of
certainty. I no longer need to have a rigid set of beliefs or a
strong faith in any one school of thought to guide my life.

Along with wrestling through how to identify myself
after leaving Christianity, I have also spent time wondering

about the nature of divinity itself. Maybe there is a different way of conceptualizing the Divine that I could explore. In truth, there are other concepts of God within Christian theology that attempt to be more encompassing. I listened to a fascinating podcast by Rob Bell in which he interviews theologian Pete Rollins.[65] Together, they discussed Paul Tillich, who was a Christian existentialist philosopher and who described the idea of God as the "ground of being." That the basest level of conscious existence is this idea of God, and all *being* arises from God. According to this theory, God is not an object (a person or thing that can be experienced through our senses) but rather is what you discover in others. When you love someone, you are loving God.

The idea of God as *being* itself seemed like a decent new framework to try, but how do I pray to *being* itself? I don't know how to interact with a God who isn't essentially a person or other conscious entity. Bell and Rollins went through a variety of approaches for thinking about who God is, including three ways of looking at God in addition to this "ground of being" idea. Rollins discussed how one might think of God as a "super-being," basically a human-like person but better than humans in every regard. Humans are flawed; super-God is perfect. Humans are finite; super-God is infinite. Humans can only be in one place at one time; super-God is omnipresent and outside of time. Humans have limited knowledge; super-God is omniscient. This is how I conceptualized God for most of my Christian life. I thought of God as basically a person, someone I could talk to and interact with, not all that different from Zeus.

Another concept that Rollins and Bell teased out was God as "hyper-being." This framework deals with God in the language of poetry and mysticism. We might use analogies like "God is love" or "God is breath." We liken the idea of God to concepts such as justice, peace, or compassion. We use analogies, referring to God as our Mother or our Father and all that those roles entail. According to Rollins, this concept defines God as "that which none greater can be conceived."

There are divine parallels for this idea across cultures and religions. In the ancient Hebrew language, the name for God was *Yahweh*, which Bell reports was thought to be trying to mimic the sound of breathing: *Yah* (inhale), *Weh* (exhale).[66] God as breath; God as life itself. God even named godself "I am," the state of being, in the Bible.[67] In *Braiding Sweetgrass*, Robin Wall Kimmerer discusses the indigenous word "*yawe*—the animate to be." Anyone possessed of life and spirit would be described using the word *yawe*. As I learned from a tour guide during our trip to Kauai, the word *Hawaii* can be broken up into *ha*, meaning "breath of life," *wai* meaning "water" or "life force," and *'i*, their word for God, again linking breath and life itself to God. Hindus practice yoga, in which *prana*, or the breath of life, is stretched and expanded through yogic poses, or *asanas*.[68] Chinese culture focuses on *qi* or *chi*, which literally translates as "air" or "breath" and refers to the vital life force within us. Buddhists use breath to keep them grounded in the present moment. Breath is seen around the world as connected to the Divine. This all fits into that framework of God as hyper-being—God is breath or life itself.

The last concept Bell and Rollins discussed in the podcast defines God as *event*. In this theology God isn't a person or object but rather an event or a process. "God is the name we give to that which calls us to great love, freedom, democracy, and hospitality."[69] In other words, when we love someone and are moved to compassion for them, that act of love and compassion is God. When we work to bring more freedom to others, that work of liberation is God. When we honor the inherent dignity and value of another human being, even when we disagree or don't fully understand them—that behavior and attitude is God. I was most drawn to this idea and laughed when they identified this theory as the most atheistic of the four frameworks.

My pastor, during our discussion of all my spiritual questions and doubts, told me about one theory that God may be part of dark matter. Dark matter and dark energy are poorly understood but attempt to answer the question of why the universe continues to expand since it shouldn't be according to our understanding of gravity. Dark energy and dark matter make up 95% of the universe and are a component of "empty" space that isn't empty at all.[70] Perhaps God is part of this dark energy/matter that is a driving force behind the expansion of space, the thing responsible for holding us all together. If so, God isn't all that different from gravity: an invisible, omnipresent force that is constantly working for our betterment by holding everything together. I don't worship gravity, so why would I worship God?

Richard Rohr, a Franciscan priest, says that God is not so much *a* Being as *being* itself.[71] That the state of being—of existing, of being alive—*is* God, much like the "God as the ground of being" theology. This makes any living creature divine and part of God. In this scenario, I am God, my neighbor is God, trees in my yard are God, immigrants and refugees are God, politicians are God, my patients at work are God, my friend's dog is God. God is part of every living thing. This view makes me want to treat them all with dignity and respect and inspires me to want to take better care of our planet and all its creatures.

This sounds nice until you think about horrible people. How could they be God too? Does that mean Hitler was part of God? Perhaps every living being is capable of both good and evil all the time, and God is not a state of perfection. There is an argument to be made that even the God in the Christian Bible wasn't perfect. Apparently that God thought they messed up so badly in creating the Earth that they attempted to wipe out everything with a flood and start over, committing mass genocide and saving just one family.[72] Then after all that, God ordered their people to enslave others and commit genocides themselves on peoples who occupied the land that they now wanted,[73] all before Jesus, as the human representation of that God, eventually demonstrated nonviolence and radical love for one's enemy.[74] Did this God mature and become a better version of themselves over time? I am certainly not perfect myself, but I am drawn to the idea that the *state of being alive* is divine, that any living creature that contains the breath of life is divine. I like this idea after learning more about evolution and how deeply related and connected we all are, every living thing a distant branch on the shared Tree of Life. If we truly valued all living things as divine, I think we would see far fewer environmental problems, fewer wars, and fewer abuses of humans and animals. If every living thing was divine, how much better would we be inspired to treat each other? The *yah-weh*, the *ha*, the *prana* is part of all of creation and connects us all.

I heard a beautiful story about the nature of consciousness in which our lives and our individual selves are compared to drops of ocean spray flying through the air. For a moment we are distinct, solitary drops of water, enjoying the world with all our senses—feeling the wind whip past, smelling the sea, looking out at the horizon, hearing the crash of the surf or caw of the gulls—and then we fall back into the ocean. Now we are no longer individual drops with our own senses, thoughts, and consciousness, but a small and indistinguishable part of the entire ocean. My Sarah-Henn-Hayward drop of water is flying in the sea spray, and I'm trying my best to enjoy the ride before I fall back into the ocean.

If only we could act like one big, happy, messed up, argumentative, and loving family. I know plenty of families are dysfunctional and beyond, but in relatively healthy families, even when conflicts come up and fights break out, we usually maintain a level of love, respect, and dignity shown to each other. We give our families the benefit of the doubt and allow space for second (and third, fourth, tenth) chances.

IT FEELS MUCH EASIER FOR me, at this point, to do away with the concept of God entirely rather than come up with these convoluted, highly theological, and confusing concepts that don't really make sense. I find a world without God to make the most sense, though I try to withhold judgment. But the only guarantee I see in life is this actual moment. All I know for certain is that I am here, now (though there are fun philosophical debates about even this). I don't know much about the distant past, and I know nothing about the future. But I do exist right now, and I am surrounded by my family, my friends, my community, my nation, and the entire human race. I am guaranteed this moment and this moment only, with no reliable promises about what happens next.

So I had better make the most of each moment.

I had better do my best to live a fulfilling, rewarding, satisfying life.

THROUGHOUT MY SPIRITUAL REVOLUTION I felt a strong pull to the outdoors. When I was laid off at the onset of the pandemic, I went on long, meaningful walks in the woods near my neighborhood. Sunshine, the resultant vitamin D, and the burst of endorphins from exercising did their best to keep me from sliding into depression at finding myself and the world in such a sad state.

I looked to the wisdom of the established Ponderosa Pines and the fleeting beauty of the spring balsamroot flowers for life lessons. Nature taught me the dual truths that beauty and joy and pain and suffering may be short-lived and that our lives are long enough to withstand wild weather and bough-bending storms. A year later I felt loving caresses from the wind blowing through my hair while riding my bike to work at my new job, no longer imagining the Holy Spirit to be sending me love and support but feeling it the same. I now recognized that I am a creature of this planet like all else, as equally deserving of love and affection as the adorable sea otters holding each other's paws while they sleep.

I share an ancient ancestry with trees and flowers, with orcas and orangutans, and with every person who has ever walked this beautiful planet. I am a part of nature, and nature is a part of me. I feel *related* to nature in a way that I never have before. I used to think humans were separate, special, and above the rest of creation, but now I feel intricately linked to everything around me. It's beautiful.

I had a profound experience of this connectedness that is so difficult to explain with words. I was doing yoga in the beautiful Cathedral of St. John the Evangelist in Spokane. The diocese opened the church to the greater community for "Yoga at the Cathedral" once a month, and it became hugely popular. Cathedrals were designed to inspire awe, to make us feel small and insignificant compared to the soaring arches and buttresses to put us in a worshipful spirit.

Even without believing in God, I found the effect is the same.

Beautiful architecture and rainbow reflections from the colorful stained glass will always be aesthetically pleasing and inspiring. At the end of the yoga routine, the instructor had everyone sit in Padmasana, or lotus pose, and led us through three "Oms." There were over a hundred people present. The reverberation of everyone's voice making the same sound filled the nave with a steady hum that made all the molecules in the air and in my body vibrate at the same frequency. The sense of connection overwhelmed me.

That sense of connection only became stronger since leaving God behind, especially when I am out in nature.

I used to give God credit for every beautiful natural scene I was blessed to behold, used to praise God for sunny days and for rain when it was needed, used to hear God's whisper on the wind. As my understanding of the world drastically changed, I realized that all the things I love about nature exist independently of any Divine Creator. Nature is inherently beautiful because it exists, not because anyone made it to be beautiful for my eyes to enjoy. I am sheerly lucky to get to live on such a pretty planet, lucky to have the time and resources to travel and explore spectacular places, lucky to feel connected to all of creation when walking in the great outdoors.

Nature is beautiful, powerful, terrifying, majestic, challenging, and peaceful all on its own. From glacial lakes along the Continental Divide to window-rattling thunderstorms, from the crashing roar of the ocean to town-leveling tornadoes, from pristine beaches to mountain peaks too tempting not to climb, from walking through a sun-dappled forest to swinging gently in my backyard hammock while a breeze makes the leaves dance overhead—I love nature. It's the closest thing to a replacement for God that I've found. Nature tempts me, inspires me, humbles me, teaches me, centers me, and pushes me to be greater.

With nature I feel at home in my own tiny but special place to belong. With the warmth of the sun on my face, the smell of the earth in my nose, and the sound of all my distant cousins flitting, flying, and scampering around—I am in church. I feel connected to all who came before me and concerned about future generations to come thanks to this moment of massive global climate change, yet at the same time, getting outside and feeling the soft moss and warm earth under my feet calms my spirit in a way that feels divine.

The Earth has withstood millions of years of chaos and change. No matter what happens next, nature will prevail.

Living

THERE IS A POSTER HANGING in my kitchen that spells out our family creed. I read a book by Bruce Feiler called *The Secrets of Happy Families* in which he discusses the benefits of developing a family-wide identity and mission. I took that to heart, and we made a creed.

Our creed states that my family values a curious and open-handed approach to faith; that we treat each other with love and respect and build family traditions; that we maintain an attitude of kindness, humility, optimism, and playfulness; that we celebrate intellectual curiosity; that we pursue our interests and gifts with vulnerability, courage, and dedication; that we take full responsibility for our decisions and their consequences; that we value experiences over things; that we seek to serve and defend others with generosity and without judgment; and that we strive to preserve and respect the environment and own our role within it. Most of these values came to my husband and me under the banner of our Christian faith; the rest came from Brené Brown.

Here's the thing: I can value all those things without needing the gift of heaven or the threat of hell to motivate me. I can still strive to behave in those ways whether I think a god will reward me or not. I think Jesus's story and teaching are a great way to strive to be, with or without him being a deity or even real.

I know the Bible gets appropriated, abused, and misinterpreted constantly, and yet the Bible I learned about has beautiful lessons within. I studied the life of Jesus within the culture of his day, and I was thrilled to learn that he was radical in his treatment of women. He had female apostles and female financial backers, and he spoke to women as equals, bestowing them with dignity and value in a world that denied them those things. The newly resurrected Jesus chose to first appear to a woman and trusted her to be the first one to tell others of his return. He was radically inclusive of ethnic minorities, the "untouchables," societal lowlifes, the disabled, the unhealthy, and the mentally ill.

While studying the Bible, I also learned that Jesus eschewed material wealth, reserving harsh words for the rich and powerful. I was actually frightened of his teachings on wealth: simply by being an American, I am a member of the global wealthy elite, and Jesus made it sound damn near impossible for the wealthy to enter heaven. When the rich man asked Jesus what to do to achieve salvation, he was told to give away all his riches, a sacrifice he couldn't bear to make.[75]

Money is a complicated topic, and I don't think striving to earn a good living is wrong. Nor do I think it's wrong to make a lot of money and be able to afford to go on exotic vacations or buy a speedboat. I do think society has placed too much importance on money and, along with our warped scarcity mindset, has created massive problems from wealth inequality. It does seem immoral for a single person to possess billions of dollars while millions of others are suffering from basic problems that money would easily solve. Nuance is needed to have a healthy relationship with money, and saying "rich is bad" is a bit too black and white for my liking. I appreciate, however, that Jesus upended the social value that "rich is good" and caused people to think.

Jesus railed against going along with the power structures of his day. He modeled a bare minimum of respect for authority and certainly not blind submission. Jesus wasn't patriotic or particularly supportive of the religious leaders from his own faith. When he was asked about paying taxes, you can practically hear the "pft" between the lines: "Render to Caesar the things that are Caesar's, and to God the things that are God's."[76] Caesar wants these coins? This earthly money that's here one day and gone the next? Sure, why not. God wants your character, your behavior, your love, your soul. Jesus's focus was on warning us about the dangers of religiosity and hypocrisy, of performative morality and inner corruption. His message was dangerous to a society built on a powerful elite class controlling the masses. It caused corrupt politicians to come clean.[77] It caused religious leaders to be held to higher standards and not take advantage of their power.[78] It caused people to give away their wealth and abandon their societally acceptable aspirations, no longer swayed by the gods of greed, power, and acquisition.[79] Today, Jesus's attitude towards wealth and materialism would get him crucified on Wall Street in a heartbeat.

But Jesus's message was freeing: he offered people a way to live that didn't follow society's rules. And he offered this to everyone—people from his own religion and culture, foreigners and "heathens," men and women, the famous and the lowest of the low. The Jesus I learned about did not care about labels—labels of religion, gender, ethnicity, or otherwise. He loved the individual people he met regardless of how they identified themselves, regardless of how hard they were working to improve their own lives, regardless of how well they behaved. He met people where they were at, and because of that total acceptance and love they were drawn to him and motivated to better themselves. The Jesus I knew would, I think, be horrified to see how many of his followers live, and vote, and use their time and money today.

I don't think the world has ever come close to following Jesus's teachings on the whole, but I would love to see that day arrive. I think we truly would be better off if people lived out the principles and values taught by Jesus. This isn't meant to trick anyone into considering Christianity, and yes, I'm sure it seems strange for me to be talking about Jesus so much in the later part of this book when I no longer believe in the whole concept of God. To be clear, I don't think Jesus had an exclusive grasp on this way to be human. These values can be found in other religions and schools of thought, and I would equally recommend those to you, but I am simply not educated enough in other worldviews to discuss them adequately. Christianity is my native language, so that is what I must work with.

Emergent truth is still truth. Even if there is no fundamental reality to the nature of God, some of the concepts of spirituality and religion are still useful paradigms with which to parse the world. The lessons I learned from my brand of Christianity provide a nice blueprint for being a fully realized, communal, socially responsible human, and thinking—as I do now—that this current life is all we will ever know, I am more motivated than ever to live the best life possible and be the best kind of human I can be.

While I can see that believing the world to be godless and without final judgment could cause some folks to go hedonistic, I don't think that is a healthy approach to living. I've seen enough films and read enough books to know that living for yourself alone and putting pleasure above all else is not satisfying in the long run. It doesn't feel good to be selfish all the time. Or maybe it does to some folks, but my morality meter is too rigged to care about others for me to change on that deep of a level.

When I first got to college, I jumped right into the drinking scene to get that full American collegiate experience. I was out every weekend at house parties, pregaming in my dorm room with my roommates, and drunkenly roaming the streets around campus looking for the next, best party. But there was one evening I remember going straight out without pregaming ahead of time. Arriving stone-sober on the party scene was a depressing experience. Folks had already puked in bushes, passed out on the sidewalks, and generally looked stupid as they danced and tried to make human connections the way only idiotic college students know how to do. It really turned me off, and I knew then that drinking myself into bliss would never be a thing.

I remained a prude all my life (purity culture had its way with me) and never had sex until I married my husband, so I cannot speak to the glory or emptiness of one-night stands. I've heard that they are *potentially* unsatisfying and less enjoyable than sex with someone you know and respect and even love. I did have my tame version of hook-ups, making out with strangers in bars in Milwaukee and clubs in Australia, and that sure was fun! And, at the same time, I would have never wanted to continue living that way forever and miss out on the experience of being in a healthy, loving, committed relationship as I currently am.

I was never too tempted by drugs. In my party phase, I dabbled with marijuana, but I certainly wouldn't want to get high every day of my life. Stronger drugs scare the crap out of me. It seems to me that a temporary blissed-out experience is certainly not worth the price of addiction and all the messy harm that causes to everyone within a 500-mile radius.

All this to say, hedonism may be a fun phase, but I cannot imagine it to be an ultimately rewarding or satisfying way to live. On the other hand, I sympathize with folks who believe in a godless, pointless world and become nihilistic. Nihilism is the idea that nothing matters and everything is meaningless, and technically, in an eternal sense, I agree. But as Sean Carroll showed me with poetic naturalism, just because the universe is pointless and random on a fundamental level doesn't mean that everything is meaningless in our day-to-day lives. Our actions and interactions matter to the people in our lives, to our own health and happiness, and to our broader communities. Our specific lives matter during our lifetimes even if they won't be remembered or rewarded in the afterlife.

So my attitude toward living now is one of emphasizing enjoyment while remaining a responsible, functional member of society. I feel inspired that this is my only chance at consciousness and grateful that I am living the life I am today. I feel more grateful than ever for my friends, my husband, my kids, and my family, and I am grateful for the natural environment I'm surrounded by in the Pacific Northwest. There is so much beauty around me, and I'm taking it for granted less often. I glance over at the sun shining on the hills and lighting up the evergreens while the morning mist streams through their needles as I ride my bike to work, and I feel elated.

I also feel more motivated to stay present and make the most of each moment. I keep going to work, juggle the kids' schedules, and keep up with the constant mental chatter involved in managing a household. I still go through the daily grind, but I am able to find more moments of beauty, joy, appreciation, and humor. I catch myself laughing harder and more often these days. My husband makes me laugh, my kids make me laugh, patients at work make me laugh, and Instagram makes me laugh. My feed is mainly full of comedians, with social activists, uplifting news accounts, and friends filling out the rest. My son has a favorite Instagram account that I mistakenly showed him in which people fall in comical ways, and we giggle over that at least once a week.

Parts of my life feel different now. For instance, I am no longer afraid of swearing. That old guilt complex I carried around from my upbringing about swearing held a tight grip, and I clearly recall the moment it clicked in my mind when I realized that I no longer believed a god was listening to anything I thought or said anymore. And shitfuckhotdamn that's been cathartic and fun to explore!

One of the worst parts of losing my faith has been the struggle to stay optimistic. It's harder to believe that everything will work out in the end when I no longer imagine God crashing through and destroying evil at some point in the future. Along with that, I've had more anxiety when taking risks. I used to pray for safety before doing anything adventurous or risky, and now I feel the risks more acutely. God isn't my lifeguard anymore, watching from the wings and ready to step in and save me if needed.

While getting ready for our recent family trip to Glacier, I found myself growing legitimately scared about a bear attacking us. We had gone in October when the bears were in their last efforts to fatten up before hibernation and the park was practically empty. We had planned to hike in the woods with two tasty little kids whose cheeks and toe-toes I threaten to eat every day—of course a bear would want to have a bite! I got so worked up thinking about a bear coming after my kids that I actually considered canceling our hikes. I've never been that anxious about an adventurous activity before. But without God, I felt so vulnerable. Which is the reality I suppose. However, I rallied: we were smart, carried bear spray, and gave the kids whistles that they blew obnoxiously during the entire hike, so we weren't sneaking up on anything within a one-mile radius. Things worked out, but I found myself missing the comfort blanket of prayer when my vulnerability was on full display.

Overall, not much has really changed since leaving Christianity on a day-to-day basis. I keep reading books about all things spiritual because it is a topic that still interests me. I'm digging deeper into other schools of thought, learning more about Taoism and Sufi mysticism. I came across the writing of Reza Aslan, a scholar of the sociology of religion, and I obsessively read his books on the history of humanity's conceptions of God and of the historical figure of Jesus.[80] I continue to value the same things, treat others the way I would want to be treated, try to raise my kids to be good humans, and engage with societal issues. I still see all the suffering and evil in the world, and especially now that I am without the comfort of knowing others will have an eternal reward for their earthly misery, I am highly motivated to do whatever small part I can to lighten their burdens. Even without a heavenly reward looming in the distance, there are still real reasons altruism feels good, not the least being that we get an emotional payoff for helping others because it contributes to the survival of the species.

For now, I'm content to take the lessons and values I gleaned from Christianity and continue to apply those to my life as it feels right. I think that loving others as yourself is a great goal. I think being wary of cultural messaging and questioning whether I truly want what society is saying I should want is a great way to assess the world. I think that humans are meant for community and do better when we live openly and honestly with a group of trusted individuals, whether born-family or found-family. I think that looking out for "the least of these"[81] and helping our fellow humans in need of assistance is beautiful. I think that personal responsibility, humility, generosity, and love are great guiding principles, and I will continue to strive to follow them.

WHILE I WAS STUDYING ABROAD, I took a class called "Experiencing the Australian Landscape." No joke, I earned college credits for going camping with forty adventurous students from around the world on both a four-day backpacking trip and a four-day canoe trip in southern Australia. Each experience was incredible, but the canoe excursion on the Murray River left an imprint on my mind that makes me both wince and smile.

Everything started off on a great note. After leaving campus and driving to a launch site on the river, we were all paired up and loaded our gear for the weekend into the hulls of the canoes. My partner and I were both reasonably fit, so we quickly paddled to the front of the pack, the sun shining on our faces, urging us forward. We had driven several hours to get to the river, so we only had time to put in a few miles that first afternoon before stopping to set up camp for the night. There were four American girls on this trip, myself included, so we all bunked up in an oversized tent and made quick use of our stores of chocolaty snacks and boxed wine. Laughter and stories filled our tent late into the night.

The next morning greeted us bright and early, and we struggled to make breakfast with cold-stiffened fingers. We would need our fuel that morning as we had close to twenty-five miles to paddle that day to reach our next stop. Now, our campsite was essentially just an open area on the bank of the river, not an actual campground; there were absolutely no amenities. We splashed some river water on our faces, found thick enough trees behind which to do our morning business out of sight of the rest of the class, and reapplied our deodorant. I was used to roughing it, but some of the girls in the group found the idea of releasing their bowels under the wide-open sky totally appalling. The question of the day became, "Have you pooped under a tree yet?" Classy.

Everyone launched into the water in high spirits, ready for our first full day on the river. I had to pinch myself several times along the way to be sure I wasn't dreaming. There were wild flocks of cockatoos racing past us by the hundreds, and their exotic calls and feathery mohawks beckoned us along. Grateful to stop for lunch, we all rested and recuperated on the riverbank in preparation for the afternoon haul. That evening, our shoulders burning, we stopped a little early at one of the few places with easy access to the shore for all our canoes. Worlds collided around the campfire that night as classmates from Japan, Holland, Australia, and Germany swapped stories and told tales from home. The American girls' tent was much quieter that night as we all collapsed into our sleeping bags.

Day three: up bright and early again. A little stiff and sore from the previous day's activities. Another twenty-five miles to go. No sun. As we unzipped our tent, we were slapped in the face with a bitter wind and threatened by an overcast sky. We had no choice but to pack up camp, even as the rain started to fall, and hit the water. We were paddling *into* the wind: not a fun task when it was whipping needle-sharp, icy raindrops on our faces. My partner and I felt like we were on a watery treadmill, furiously paddling forward and barely stopping ourselves from getting blown backward. At one point, the rain mixed with tears of frustration and pain in a salty, slushy mess on my face.

To this day, I don't know how we did it. I honestly did not think we would be able to make the distance required for the day and would need the bus to find a closer spot to pick us up. But our professor and teacher's aide were more than encouraging, and they took turns swapping partners with some of the weaker boats so no one fell too far behind. My partner was paired with one of the weakest girls in the group and basically muscled through the storm by herself, an act of endurance and strength I could only admire.

My new partner was a young man from Germany, and as he did not speak English fluently, we resigned ourselves to shrugging our shoulders to communicate before pushing on. The only German words I knew were cuss words gleaned from friends who took German in high school, which did come in handy as we commiserated about the *scheißen* day. Somehow we paddled the rest of the mileage needed to get us within an easy distance of our pick-up location for the next morning.

We stumbled into our tents that night, no energy left for the slightest chit-chat or giggle. Fatigue seeped into my bones. Sleeping on the cold, hard ground in my thin sleeping bag felt like lying on a downy bed in a five-star hotel. I was out cold within seconds of my head hitting the bag.

On the final morning, the weather improved, the sun returned, and we had an easy paddle across a large, marshy lake where the river opened and spread out. After a mere five miles we pulled up on shore and were greeted by our bus driver. I had to restrain myself from planting a big wet kiss on his cheek. I was so grateful to be done with that exhausting trip. On the four-hour drive back to campus on the (stinky) bus, I never felt more accomplished in my entire life.

To this day the memory shines in my mind as one of the proudest moments of my life. I have now given birth to two eight-plus pound children without pain medication, and I might still consider the canoe trip the more impressive feat. That weekend was hardly the most fun I had ever had; we were not in the most beautiful location I had ever seen, and it was not the wildest experience I had ever been a part of. It was draining, challenging, and at times full of despair. Yet I became a better person for persevering and pushing on. My resolve strengthened, and the sheer joy I felt after accomplishing such a daunting task was overwhelming.

Nature can be a cruel teacher and coach, taunting and beautiful in one moment and vicious and deadly in the next.

But after enduring this trial and coming out literally stronger on the other side, I am emboldened. I learned what I am capable of, what storms I can weather, what challenges I can overcome. Nature inspires the courage I need to overcome new obstacles and persist through difficulty. I am forever grateful.

Leaping Forward

SINCE CEASING TO BELIEVE THAT God is real and walking away from the Christian faith, I feel a deep sense of peace (aside from my existential dread over climate change, but hey, God wasn't doing anything about that anyway). Not without grief and moments of confusion and loss. Not without cost, as my marriage is now in unexplored, unexpected territory that we are still learning how to navigate. But overall I feel a deeper peace than I have ever known before.

I'm at peace, and I am full of rage. I feel incandescent joy—and profound despair. I am content, and I am restless. I am full of gratitude, and I feel deep longing. I feel everything—because I am a human being. Sometimes I feel all those things in a four-minute period. Sometimes I spend a whole day in rage over some social injustice or political kerfuffle. Other days I live in peaceful gratitude for my sweet kids. The entire panorama of the atlas of the heart, to borrow from Brené Brown, is within my own heart. I am human, every single day, and I am more than okay with that.

Part of being human includes living in community with others. Nowadays, I'd argue we're even more dependent on each other than we were in our hunter/gatherer days, only we don't even know who is helping us. I don't grow, pick, or process my own food. I don't make my own clothes. I don't generate the electricity or wireless internet I am currently relying on to type this book. I certainly needed someone else to make the laptop for me. I rely on strangers to provide for most of my basic needs (for a price).

Childbirth is still dangerous—I nearly died giving birth to my son, so I can attest to this personally. Without skilled medical professionals right there with me as I labored and strangers who donated blood out of pure goodwill, I would have bled to death. I rely on others now for childcare and cleaning help to return to work and maintain the household while raising kids and keeping my sanity.

We are meant to live with others.

The lie of independence, of self-reliance, of the self-made man threatens one of the very things that makes us human. Isolationism, tribalism, fierce independence: these things make us weak, not strong. It's not a sign of strength to bear all our burdens by ourselves. It's not a sign of strength to withhold my pain, fears, and doubts from those I love to put on a show or protect them from my reality. As the lifelong work of Brené Brown keeps proving to us repeatedly—vulnerability is strength. Being open and honest with others, needing others, depending on others—these things make us human and make us strong because we are stronger together. But it is so damn hard!

It takes courage. It's scary to open up to someone, even a dearly loved friend or family member, without knowing how they will react. Without knowing if they will be gentle with our pain, our fears, and our worry. And too often we don't react well. Too many times we jump in to fix things, to smooth it all over, to try to explain or offer empty platitudes, preferring the lie of comfort and ease to the reality that life is full of suffering. It is hard to look pain in the eye—whether our own or someone else's. But pretending pain and suffering don't exist does not solve anything.

It isn't pleasant to be honest when things are hard. It's scary to ask for help. But when we are lucky enough to have people who truly care—who see us at our best *and* at our worst and love us the same—then they can help share the burden. Their presence, their care, and possibly their resources can lighten our load. They may know information that can turn our situation around or have a connection to someone who would be the perfect resource. They may have suffered similarly and could offer a sympathetic ear and shoulder to cry on, making us feel less alone in our pain. They may simply stick around and be with us in our suffering, their loving presence itself a balm to the pain.

In 2015, after conceiving for the first time, I suffered a partial molar pregnancy. It required emergency surgery—a medical abortion. My husband and I had been trying to conceive, and I was ecstatic at that positive pregnancy test. I quickly scheduled an appointment with the midwife group I'd chosen for the first ultrasound. But during the ultrasound, my husband and I could immediately tell something was off. The tech was super quiet. She didn't point out much, seemed to take forever snapping picture after picture for the midwife to review, and then left without much of a word. We braced ourselves for bad news.

But the midwife hemmed and hawed. She wondered if I had my timing off, if perhaps I wasn't as far along as I thought. Maybe there was no heartbeat yet because it was too soon. We were to return the next week for another look. I allowed myself a flicker of hope.

Next week, second ultrasound, different midwife. This one wondered aloud why the first midwife told us to come back only one week later as two weeks would be needed to gather any more helpful information. "Come back next week." I was a zombie at work. I hope none of my patients needed sharp attention and care because my brain was constantly elsewhere.

The following week—our third appointment and ultrasound in as many weeks—the midwife on duty brought in her OB partner for a consultation. The OB called for immediate surgery, that night. We were shocked, confused, and deeply disappointed after thinking we had successfully gotten pregnant. There was a risk the situation could develop into cancer, a threat that hung over our heads for months after my surgery. There were unknown timelines about when we could safely try to conceive again. And I am *so grateful* that we had told our closest friends and family about the pregnancy before it all went to hell. They showed up with care, encouragement, meals, massages—support. Many women told me stories of similar experiences they had suffered, making me feel less alone, broken, or defective. Our people got us through an extremely difficult time feeling seen, cared for, and loved.

There's a description of the Trinity—a Christian tenet that came about during one of those ecumenical councils and is not present in the Bible—in which God the Father, Jesus the Son, and the Holy Spirit are somehow both three unique

Beings and one Being at the same time. The Christian God itself does not exist without community—never separate, never alone. I still love that image. It reminds me of the atom (yes, I'm a nerd). Atoms are made of protons, neutrons, and electrons. Three separate, independent particles that together form one unified particle, the basis for all of life. Three as one, the most basic building block of the known universe. At a fundamental-truth level, there is community.

MY ENTIRE BEDROCK HAS SHAKEN and changed, and I've come away clutching with renewed passion at certain truths. I have opened and examined every last thing I've been taught about the world, and now I have a strong sense of clarity about my life and what I want to make of it.

If I worship anything, it is Now, this present moment. I want to fight against boredom, worry, planning, and distraction to truly be present.

I worship paying attention to the vibrant colors at sunset, to the leaves dancing on the wind and the feel of my hair blowing around on my back, to my children's voices and inventive imaginations, to the laughter of my friends, to the warmth of my husband's embrace.

I worship each moment in the brief flash of my kids' childhood whenever they light up with joy or discovery, at every new skill and imagined world they create.

I worship the time I spend with my patients who are at the tail end of their journeys, listening to their stories and paying respect to the full lives they've led.

I worship not taking life for granted, my plans for the future held loosely in open hands as I go along for the ride with curiosity and wonder.

I worship Love—healthy, unconditional love for myself, for my family, for all others, even folks who annoy me or scare me or frustrate me. I am still learning what that looks like in practice and how I can love my fellow humans whom I don't particularly care for while maintaining my health and boundaries. No simple puzzle to solve there—life doesn't get any easier to navigate without religion. But even Jesus summarized the entire Hebrew scriptures simply: love God and love your neighbor as yourself.[82] At the end of a lifetime of spiritual exploration, Siddhartha said, "It seems to me that love is the most important thing in the world."[83] Islam teaches the vital importance of love, saying, "You will not enter Paradise until you believe, and you will not believe until you love one another."[84] Loving ourselves, loving others, and loving the world is what it is ultimately all about.

I also worship freedom—freedom from "shoulds," from cultural expectations and restrictions. Freedom from needing to look a certain way, dress in a certain style, talk with the right tone and popular catchphrases, and shop in the latest fashions. Freedom to grow old naturally, comfortable in my body, which is becoming more challenging—the wrinkles are coming! Freedom to revel in the strength of my body even while she doesn't look like the bodies on the magazine cover. Freedom to own my scars (both figurative and literal—my scoliosis scars are massive) and the life lessons they taught me without embarrassment. Freedom from categorizing, judging, and comparing my status to others. Freedom from comparing in any way. Freedom to let others live as they choose without trying to control or force my definitions of meaning and importance upon them.

Freedom from shame.

Freedom to be who I truly am.

Freedom to be open and vulnerable with my fellow drops of water.

I don't know what happens after this, where "I" will go when my splash rejoins the great Ocean.

But I will choose love and peace, community, kindness and joy, awe, curiosity and adventure and freedom at every chance I get.

Acknowledgments

I deeply believe that no one accomplishes anything alone. Writing a book is a classic example of community effort. This book started in the pages of my personal journal when I realized that I could no longer honestly say that I believed in God. As it poured out of me, I relied on my husband, my kids' schools, and my babysitter to provide me with windows of time to write. Lydia Mulligan took on the heaviest lifting job of all and whipped my messy, clumsy book into professional shape. Her guidance and input were invaluable. I needed early beta readers and would like to thank my friends Dawn, Haylee, Brandon, and Heather for reading the earliest, messiest version of the book and for providing feedback. I benefitted from conversations with David Morris with Lake Drive Books to learn some ins and outs about publishing before he even agreed to publish me. I relied on my editor, Stephanie Eagleson, for turning this into a real live book. I benefitted from my Uncle Tom who reached out and introduced me to his niece, Julia Soplop, who graciously gave me a copy of her book on self-publishing and made herself available for any questions I had throughout the process. This book would not exist without a lot of help from all of you wonderful people.

Heather—going over my book with you felt like an actual book club in which you read my words and took them seriously and that gave me so much confidence to move forward. Thank you.

Lydia—for the massive gift of going through my book with a developmental eye, I cannot thank you enough. You whipped the book into much better shape than it was, challenged me to add "*scene!*" to bring it to life, and encouraged me to keep going. Thanks upon thanks. I owe you many donuts.

To my editor Stephanie Eagleson—bottomless thanks for turning this book into an actual, professional book. Your notes, comments, and edits crafted this into the easily readable, compliant book that it is. I appreciate your help and am so glad to have worked with you on this project. Madeleine L'Engle fan club forever!

To my parents—thank you for raising me so well, for loving me unconditionally (even when things didn't turn out as you expected) and for supporting me throughout my life. I owe you both an enormous debt that can never be repaid.

To my kids—if you ever read this, I hope it will inspire you and encourage you to live a well-examined life, to think deeply, and to make the most of this precious gift of existence. I love you both with every cell in my body and I am so grateful for you. Cuddles and kisses.

To my husband—you are better than I could have ever hoped for. We were lucky to meet and date the way we did, and I am still discovering how truly lucky I really am. Thank you for being so good to me and for loving me and supporting me so well, even when my path took me in an unexpected direction. I admire and respect you so much, and I plan on cuddling with you for a long time to come. Living this life with you is priceless. I love you.

To you reading this little book—thank you!! I hope it resonated and helped on your own journey, challenged you to think differently, or comforted you with the knowledge that you are not alone in your beliefs (or lack thereof). Thanks for picking this book up and reading it the whole way through; words cannot express my gratitude.

Books from the Journey

Being a bookworm, I've consumed countless influential books over the years. I learned a lot from spiritual memoirs and nonfiction, and great novels have shown me truth through story. I could go way back in time and credit the influence of thought-provoking books I read way back in middle school and beyond, but then this bibliography would be longer than most of the chapters of this book. I've tried to highlight books I've read over the last fifteen years of my slow-burning deconstruction period. These are the books that stretched my perspective, challenged my views, deepened my understanding, and inspired my beliefs.

Bell, Rob. *Everything Is Spiritual: Who We Are and What We're Doing Here*. New York: St. Martin's Essentials, 2020.

Bell, Rob. *Love Wins: A Book About Heaven, Hell, and the Fate of Every Person Who Ever Lived*. New York: HarperOne, 2011.

Bell, Rob. *What Is the Bible?: How an Ancient Library of Poems, Letters, and Stories Can Transform the Way You Think and Feel about Everything*. New York: HarperOne, 2017.

Bell, Rob. *Velvet Elvis: Repainting the Christian Faith*. Grand Rapids: Zondervan, 2005.

Bessey, Sarah. *Jesus Feminist: An Invitation to Revisit the Bible's View of Women*. New York: Howard Books, 2013.

Bessey, Sarah. *Out of Sorts: Making Peace with an Evolving Faith.* New York: Howard Books, 2015.

Bessey, Sarah. *Miracles and Other Reasonable Things: A Story of Unlearning and Relearning God.* New York: Howard Books, 2019.

Blakeslee, Nate. *American Wolf: A True Story of Survival and Obsession in the West.* New York: Broadway Books, 2018.

Bolz-Weber, Nadia. *Accidental Saints: Finding God in All the Wrong People.* New York: The Crown Publishing Group, 2016.

Brown, Austin Channing. *I'm Still Here: Black Dignity in a World Made for Whiteness.* New York: Convergent, 2018.

Carroll, Sean. *The Big Picture: On the Origins of Life, Meaning, and the Universe Itself.* New York: Penguin Random House, 2017.

Claiborne, Shane and Chris Haw. *Jesus for President: Politics for Ordinary Radicals.* Grand Rapids: Zondervan, 2008.

Claiborne, Shane and Jim Wallis. *The Irresistible Revolution: Living as an Ordinary Radical.* Grand Rapids: Zondervan, 2006.

Coates, Ta-Nehisi. *Between the World and Me.* New York: Spiegel and Grau, 2015.

Collins, Francis S. *The Language of God: A Scientist Presents Evidence for Belief.* New York: Free Press, 2007.

Curtice, Kaitlin B. *Native: Identity, Belonging, and Rediscovering God.* Grand Rapids: Brazos Press, 2020.

Davis, Cynthia Vacca. *Intersexion: A Story of Faith, Identity, and Authenticity.* Grand Rapids: Lake Drive Books, 2022.

DeSilva, Jeremy. *First Steps: How Upright Walking Made Us Human.* New York: HarperCollins, 2021.

Doidge, Norman, M.D. *The Brain That Changes Itself: Stories of Personal Triumph from the Frontiers of Brain Science.* New York: Penguin Books, 2007.

Dunbar-Ortiz, Roxanne. *An Indigenous Peoples' History of the United States*. Beacon Press: Boston, 2014.

Enns, Peter. *How the Bible Actually Works: In Which I Explain How an Ancient, Ambiguous, and Diverse Book Leads Us to Wisdom Rather Than Answers—and Why That's Great News*. San Francisco: HarperOne, 2019.

Evans, Rachel Held. *A Year of Biblical Womanhood: How a Liberated Woman Found Herself Sitting on Her Roof, Covering Her Head, and Calling Her Husband Master*. Nashville: Thomas Nelson, 2012.

Grann, David. *Killers of the Flower Moon: The Osage Murders and the Birth of the FBI*. New York: Vintage Books, 2018.

Gregory, Dick. *Defining Moments in Black History: Reading Between the Lies*. New York: Amistad, 2018.

Greyson, Bruce, M.D. *After: A Doctor Explores What Near-Death Experiences Reveal about Life and Beyond*. New York: St. Martin's Essentials, 2021.

Hand, David J. *The Improbability Principle: Why Coincidences, Miracles, and Rare Events Happen Every Day*. New York: Scientific American and Farrar, Straus, and Giroux, 2014.

Harari, Yuval Noah. *Sapiens: A Brief History of Humankind*. Toronto: McClelland & Stewart, 2015.

Harper, Lisa Sharon. *The Very Good Gospel: How Everything Wrong Can Be Made Right*. Colorado Springs: WaterBrook Press, 2016.

Harvey, Jennifer. *Raising White Kids: Bringing Up Children in a Racially Unjust America*. Nashville: Abingdon Press, 2019.

Hatmaker, Jen. *Fierce, Free, and Full of Fire: The Guide to Being Glorious You*. Nashville: Nelson Books, 2020.

Hatmaker, Jen. *For the Love: Fighting for Grace in a World of Impossible Standards*. Nashville: Nelson Books, 2015.

Jacobs, Harriet. *Incidents in the Life of a Slave Girl*. Boston: self-published, 1861.

Jerkins, Morgan. *This Will Be My Undoing: Living at the Intersection of Black, Female, and Feminist in (White) America*. New York: Harper Perennial, 2018.

Khan-Cullors, Patrisse and Asha Bandele. *When They Call You a Terrorist: A Black Lives Matter Memoir*. New York: St. Martin's Griffin, 2020.

Kimmerer, Robin Wall. *Braiding Sweetgrass: Indigenous Wisdom, Scientific Knowledge, and the Teachings of Plants*. Minneapolis: Milkweed Editions, 2013.

L'Engle, Madeleine. *A Circle of Quiet*. San Francisco: Harper Collins, 1972.

L'Engle, Madeleine. *The Irrational Season*. San Francisco: HarperCollins, 1977.

L'Engle, Madeleine. *Two-Part Invention: The Story of a Marriage*. San Francisco: HarperCollins, 1988.

Masson, Jeffrey Moussaieff and Susan McCarthy. *When Elephants Weep: The Emotional Lives of Animals*. New York: Delta, 1995.

Maye, Marilyn Allman, Harold S. Buchanan, Jannette O. Domingo, Joyce Frisby Baynes, Marilyn Holifield, Myra E. Rose, Bridget Van Gronigen Warren, and Aundrea White Kelley. *Seven Sisters and a Brother: Friendship, Resistance, and Untold Truths behind Black Student Activism in the 1960s*. Coral Gables: Books & Books Press, 2021.

Nutt, Amy Ellis. *Becoming Nicole: The Transformation of an American Family*. New York: Penguin Random House, 2016.

Oluo, Ijeoma. *So You Want to Talk about Race*. New York: Seal Press, 2019.

Polkinghorne, John C. *Belief in God in an Age of Science*. New Haven: Yale University Press, 1998.

Preston, Richard. *The Wild Trees: A Story of Passion and Daring.* New York: Random House Trade Paperbacks, 2007.

Rohr, Richard. *The Universal Christ: How a Forgotten Reality Can Change Everything We See, Hope For, and Believe.* New York: Convergent, 2019.

Saad, Layla F. *Me and White Supremacy: Combat Racism, Change the World, and Become a Good Ancestor.* Naperville, IL: Sourcebooks, 2020.

Salman, Ayser. *The Wrong End of the Table: A Mostly Comic Memoir of a Muslim Arab American Woman Just Trying to Fit In.* New York: Skyhorse Publishing, 2019.

Vines, Matthew. *God and the Gay Christian: The Biblical Case in Support of Same-Sex Relationships.* New York: Convergent Books, 2014.

Watts, Alan. *The Spirit of Zen: A Way of Life, Work, and Art in the Far East.* New York: Grove Press, 1958.

Wohlleben, Peter. *The Hidden Life of Trees: What They Feel, How They Communicate—Discoveries from a Secret World.* Vancouver: Greystone Books, 2016.

Wolff, Catherine. *Beyond: How Humankind Thinks about Heaven.* New York: Riverhead Books, 2021.

Wilkerson, Isabel. *The Warmth of Other Suns: The Epic Story of America's Great Migration.* New York: Random House, 2010.

Wilkerson, Isabel. *Caste: The Origins of Our Discontents.* New York: Random House, 2020.

Yancey, Philip. *The Jesus I Never Knew.* Grand Rapids: Zondervan Publishing House, 1995.

Endnotes

1. Matthew 25:31–46.
2. Genesis 1:31.
3. Romans 3:10.
4. 1 Corinthians 10:13.
5. Madeleine L'Engle, *Two-Part Invention: The Story of a Marriage* (San Francisco: Harper Collins, 1988), introduction.
6. Romans 8:38–39.
7. John 14:6.
8. "The Archangel Gabriel," Internet Archive, last modified August 28, 2017, https://archive.org/stream/Archangel_ Gabriel_by_Lev_Tolstoy/Archangel%20Gabriel%20- 20Lev%20Tolstoy_djvu.txt.
9. "Evangelical Free Church of America," Britannica, accessed June 24, 2022, https://www.britannica.com/topic/Evangelical- Free-Church-of-America.
10. Dora B. Goldstein, "Biological Basis of Sexual Orientation" (Public lecture, Stanford's Medical Center's Lesbian-Gay Bisexual Community, Standford University, Standford, CA, March 9, 1995). https://news.stanford.edu/pr/95/950310Arc5328.html.
11. Brandon Ambrosio, "The Invention of 'Heterosexuality,'" BBC, last modified March 15, 2017, https://www.bbc.com/ future/article/20170315-the-invention-of-heterosexuality.
12. Matthew Vines, *God and the Gay Christian* (New York: Convergent Books, 2014), 31–33; 35–36; 38–39; 60–69; 134–148.

13. Arash Fereydooni, "Do Animals Exhibit Homosexuality?" *Yale Scientific*, last modified March 14, 2022, https://www.yalescientific.org/2012/03/do-animals-exhibit-homosexuality/.

14. Sean Carroll, "Frans de Waal on Culture and Gender in Primates," April 25, 2022, in *Mindscape,* podcast audio, 17:36, https://www.preposterousuniverse.com/podcast-archives/.

15. Duane Brayboy, "Two Spirits, One Heart, Five Genders," Updated: Sep 13, 2018; Original: Sep 7, 2017, https://indiancountrytoday.com/archive/two-spirits-one-heart-five-genders.

16. "The Hijra Community and Decolonizing Gender," Asian Indian Family Wellness SEWA-AIFW, last modified June 24, 2021, https://sewa-aifw.org/the-hijra-community-and-decolonizing-gender/.

17. "Beyond Gender: Indigenous Perspectives, Muxe," LA County Natural History Museum, accessed June 9, 2022, https://nhm.org/stories/beyond-gender-indigenous-perspectives-muxe.

18. "The Third Gender and Hijras," Harvard Divinity School, accessed June 9, 2022, https://rpl.hds.harvard.edu/religion-context/case-studies/gender/third-gender-and-hijras.

19. Steven Schlozman, MD, "What Are Some of the Major Theories of Development?" The Clay Center for Developing Healthy Minds, last modified September 18, 2013, https://www.mghclaycenter.org/parenting-concerns/infants-toddlers/what-are-some-of-the-major-theories-of-development/.

20. 1 John 4:7–8.

21. Christopher Gregory Weber, "Paluxy Man – The Creationist Piltdown," National Center for Science Education, last modified January 2, 2023, https://ncse.ngo/paluxy-man-creationist-piltdown.

22. William Paley, "Natural Theology, or Evidences of the Existence and Attributes of the Deity collected from the Appearances of Nature," (London: J. Faulder; Longman and Co. Cadell and Davies, 1813).

23. Sean Carroll, *The Big Picture: On the Origins of Life, Meaning, and the Universe Itself* (New York: Penguin Random House, 2017), 290.

24. Neil deGrasse Tyson, "Neil deGrasse Tyson (astrophysicist)," interview by Dax Shepherd, December 1, 2022, in *Armchair Expert,* podcast audio, 30:37, https://armchairexpertpod.com/pods/neil-degrasse-tyson.

25. Robin Wall Kimmerer, *Braiding Sweetgrass: Indigenous Wisdom, Scientific Knowledge and the Teachings of Plants,* (Minneapolis: Milkweed Editions, 2013), 3–4.

26. Rob Bell, *What Is the Bible?: How an Ancient Library of Poems, Letters, and Stories Can Transform the Way You Think and Feel About Everything* (New York: HarperOne, 2017).

27. R. Melzack, "Pain and the neuromatrix in the brain," *Journal of Dental Education* 65 (2001): 1378–1382.

28. Okada E, Matsumoto M, Fujiwara H, Toyama Y. Disc degeneration of cervical spine on MRI in patients with lumbar disc herniation: comparison study with asymptomatic volunteers. *European Spine Journal: Official Publication of the European Spine Society, the European Spinal Deformity Society, and the European Section of the Cervical Spine Research Society.* Apr 2011;20(4):585–591.

Spielman AL, Forster BB, Kokan P, Hawkins RH, Janzen DL. Shoulder after rotator cuff repair: MR imaging findings in asymptomatic individuals – initial experience. *Radiology.* Dec 1999;213(3):705–708.

Kjaer P, Leboeuf-Yde C, Korsholm L, Sorensen JS, Bendix T. Magnetic resonance imaging and low back pain in adults: a diagnostic imaging study of 40-year-old men and women. *Spine.* May 15 2005;30 (10):1173–1180.

Silvis ML, Mosher TJ, Smetana BS, et al. High prevalence of pelvic and hip magnetic resonance imaging findings in asymptomatic collegiate and professional hockey players. *American Journal of Sports Medicine.* Apr 2011;39(4):715–721.

Munk B, Lundorf E, Jensen J. Long-term outcome of meniscal degeneration in the knee: poor association between MRI and symptoms in 45 patients followed more than 4 years. *Acta Orthopaedica Scandanavia Journal.* Feb 2004;75(1):89–92.

29. Brain Games YouTube channel, "Rubber Hand Illusion," YouTube. Filmed on June 19, 2014, https://www.youtube.com/watch?v=iPFSgLDCvAs.

30. David Bolton, "A Tale of Two Nails," Neuro Orthopaedic Institute, last modified October 10, 2019, https://www.noi-group.com/noijam/a-tale-of-two-nails/.

31. "Man Shoots Nail into Brain Without Noticing," BBC News, last modified January 21, 2012, https://www.bbc.com/news/world-us-canada-16663332/.

32. "Worldwide Cancer Data," World Cancer Research Fund International, accessed March 23, 2022, https://www.wcrf.org/cancer-trends/worldwide-cancer-data/.

33. Matthew 4:7.

34. Books such as Asha Bandele and Patrisse Cullors's *When They Call You a Terrorist,* Ta-Nehisi Coates's *Between The World and Me,* Austin Channing Brown's *I'm Still Here: Black Dignity in a World Made for Whiteness,* Jennifer Harvey's *Raising White Kids,* Dick Gregory's *Defining Moments in Black History: Reading Between the Lies,* Layla F. Saad's *Me and White Supremacy, Seven Sisters and a Brother: Friendship, Resistance, and Untold Truths Behind Black*

Student Activism in the 1960s, Ijeoma Oluo's *So You Want to Talk about Race,* Morgan Jerkins's *This Will Be My Undoing,* Ayser Salman's *The Wrong End of the Table,* Roxanne Dunbar-Ortiz's *An Indigenous Peoples' History of the United States,* and David Grann's *Killers of the Flower Moon: The Osage Murders and the Birth of the FBI,* and more all contributed to my racial education since *so much* history was skipped by my private and public education curricula.

35. Roxanne Dunbar-Ortiz, *An Indigenous Peoples' History of the United States* (Beacon Press: Boston, 2014).

36. Harriet Jacobs, *Incidents in the Life of a Slave Girl* (Boston: self-published, 1861).

37. Isabel Wilkerson, *The Warmth of Other Suns* (New York: Random House, 2010).

38. Isabel Wilkerson, *Caste* (New York: Random House, 2020).

39. David Grann, *Killers of the Flower Moon: The Osage Murders and the Birth of the FBI* (New York: Vintage Books, 2018).

40. Crystal Ponti, "America's History of Slavery Began Long Before Jamestown," History, last modified August 26, 2019, https://www.history.com/news/american-slavery-before-jamestown-1619.

41. Sam Harris, *Free Will* (New York: Free Press, 2012).

42. Adrian G. Guggisberg and Anaïs Mottaz, "Timing and awareness of movement decisions: does consciousness really come too late?" Frontiers in Human Neuroscience, July 30, 2013, 7: 385. doi: 10.3389/fnhum.2013.00385. PMID: 23966921; PMCID: PMC3746176.

43. Eamon Barrett and Grady McGregor, "Reports of forced labor are driving brands to abandon Chinese cotton," *Fortune,* July 18, 2021, https://fortune.com/2021/07/18/china-cotton-forced-labor-xinjiang/.

44. Rachel Held Evans, "Life After Evangelicalism," blog post, last modified November 14, 2016, https://rachelheldevans. com/blog/life-after-evangelicalism.

45. Mary Fairchild, "How Many Religions Are There in the World?" Learn Religions, last modified March 22, 2021, https://www.learnreligions.com/how-many-religions-are-there-in-the-world-5114658.

46. Carroll, *The Big Picture*, 388.

47. Rob Bell, *Everything Is Spiritual* (New York: St. Martin's Essentials, 2020), 210.

48. Eric Niiler, "Maybe You're Not an Atheist – Maybe You're a Naturalist Like Sean Carroll," Wired, last modified May 9, 2016, https://www.wired.com/2016/05/maybe-youre-not-atheist-maybe-youre-naturalist-like-sean-carroll/.

49. Richard Preston, "The Mysterious Lives of Giant Trees," TED2008, video, 5:45, https://www.ted.com/talks/richard_preston_the_mysterious_lives_of_giant_trees.

50. Lori Cuthbert and Douglas Main, "Orca Mother Drops Calf, After Unprecedented 17 days of Mourning," National Geographic, last modified August 13, 2018, https://www.nationalgeographic.com/animals/article/orca-mourning-calf-killer-whale-northwest-news.

51. Jeremy DeSilva, *First Steps* (New York: HarperCollins, 2021).

52. Martin Luther King Jr., "Remaining Awake Through a Great Revolution." Speech given at the National Cathedral, March 31, 1968.

53. Sonia Elks, "Slavery not a crime for almost half the countries in the world—study," Reuters, last modified February 12, 2020, https://www.reuters.com/article/us-global-slavery-law-trfn/slavery-not-acrime-for-almost-half-the-countries-in-the-world-study-idUSKBN20620R.

54. Steven Pinker, "Enlightenment Now: The Case for Reason, Science, Humanism, and Progress," (Viking, 2018), https://is.gd/LHVzmL.

55. Donna L. Hoyert, "Maternal mortality rates in the United States, 2020," CDC NCHS Health E-Stats, 2022, DOI: https://dx.doi.org/10.15620/cdc:113967.

56. Harvard School of Public Health, "Black people more than three times as likely as white people to be killed during a police encounter," PLOS ONE, published June 24, 2020, https://www.hsph.harvard.edu/news/hsph-in-the-news/blacks-whites-police-deaths-disparity/.
    See also Mapping Police Violence, last updated March 31, 2022, https://mappingpoliceviolence.org/.

57. Rebecca L. Stotzer, PhD, MSW, MS, "Data Sources Hinder Our Understanding of Transgender Murders," *American Journal of Public Health* (Sept 2017), 107(9): 1362–1363, https://doi:10.2105/AJPH.2017.303973.

58. Fannie Lou Hamer, Speech Delivered at the Founding of the National Women's Political Caucus, Washington, D.C., July 10, 1971.

59. GoodGoodGood Newspaper, "143 Most Inspiring Mister Rogers Quotes for Helpers," last modified March 19, 2022, https://www.goodgoodgood.co/articles/mr-rogers-quotes.

60. David Farrier, "Flightless Bird: Religion," May 17, 2022, in *Armchair Expert*, podcast audio, https://armchairexpertpod.com/pods/fb-religion.

61. Dina A. Lienhard, "Roger Sperry's Split Brain Experiments (1959–1968)," *Embryo Project Encyclopedia* (2017-12-27), ISSN: 1940–5030. http://embryo.asu.edu/handle/10776/13035.

62. Matthew 19:23–26.

63. Merriam-Webster Online, s.v. "Agnostic," accessed August 15, 2022, https://www.merriam-webster.com/dictionary/agnostic.

64. Carroll, *The Big Picture*, 51.

65. Rob Bell, "Pete Rollins on God Part 1," July 25, 2016, in *The Robcast*, audio, https://robbell.podbean.com/e/episode-111-pete-rollins-on-god-part-1/.

66. Rob Bell, "Breathe," NOOMA video series discussion guide, (Grand Rapids: Zondervan, 2006), 11, 17.

67. Exodus 3:13–15.

68. Holly Lebowitz Rossi, "Breath, the divine metaphor, becomes a hallmark of America's twin crisis," Religion News Service, last modified July 8, 2020, https://religionnews.com/2020/07/08/breath-the-divine-metaphor/.

69. Rob Bell, "Pete Rollins on God Part 1," *The Robcast*, 34:27, https://robbell.podbean.com/e/episode-111-pete-rollins-on-god-part-1/.

70. "Dark Energy, Dark Matter," NASA Science, accessed June 12, 2022, https://science.nasa.gov/astrophysics/focus-areas/what-is-dark-energy.

71. Richard Rohr, "God Is Being Itself," Center for Action and Contemplation, May 20, 2020, https://cac.org/daily-meditations/god-is-being-itself-2020-05-20/.

72. Genesis 7:1–4.

73. Deuteronomy 20: 16,17; 1 Samuel 15:3.

74. Matthew 5:44.

75. Matthew 19:21–22.

76. Mark 12:17.

77. Luke 5:27–28; Luke 19:1–10.

78. 1 Timothy 3:1–10; James 3:1.

79. Acts 4:32–37.

80. Reza Aslan, *God: A Human History* (New York: Random House, 2017) and Reza Aslan, *Zealot: The Life and Times of Jesus of Nazareth* (New York: Random House, 2014).
81. Matthew 25:40.
82. Matthew 22:37–38.
83. Herman Hesse, *Siddhartha* (New York: Bantam Books, 1951), 147.
84. Muslim.Sg, "Beautiful Quran Verses on Love," last modified September 1, 2020, https://muslim.sg/articles/beautiful-quran-verses-on-love.

About the Author

Sarah Henn Hayward is a writer, a voracious reader, a deep thinker, a curious learner, a nature lover, a brave adventurer, an Enneagram 7, a former Christian, a doctor of physical therapy, and a loyal friend. Her blog at sarahhennhayward. com highlights the books of marginalized communities, and she is active on Instagram as @shaywardwrites. She lives in Spokane, Washington with her husband Dan and her two children.

About Lake Drive Books

Lake Drive Books is an independent publishing company offering books that help you heal, grow, and discover.

We offer books about values and strategies, not ideologies; authors that are spiritually rich, contextually intelligent, and focused on human flourishing; and we want to help readers feel seen.

If you like this book, or any of our other books at lakedrivebooks.com, we could use your help: please follow our authors on social media or join their email newsletters, and please especially tell others about these remarkable books and their authors.

www.ingramcontent.com/pod-product-compliance
Lightning Source LLC
Chambersburg PA
CBHW031457120626
46545CB00005B/1645

* 9 7 8 1 9 5 7 6 8 7 3 0 8 *